Rhode Island College Junior Class

YEARBOOK 1899 The Grist...

Agriculture and Mechanic Arts

Rhode Island College Junior Class

YEARBOOK 1899 The Grist...
Agriculture and Mechanic Arts

ISBN/EAN: 9783741176708

Manufactured in Europe, USA, Canada, Australia, Japa

Cover: Foto ©Andreas Hilbeck / pixelio.de

Manufactured and distributed by brebook publishing software (www.brebook.com)

Rhode Island College Junior Class

YEARBOOK 1899 The Grist...

..The Grist..

Published by the Junior Class

of the

Rhode Island College

of

Agriculture and Mechanic Arts

Volume 3

Kingston, Rhode Island

June, 1899

Contents

DEDICATION.
BOARD OF EDITORS.
INTRODUCTION.
BOARD OF MANAGERS.
COLLEGE CALENDAR.
FACULTY.
COLLEGE ACTIVITY COMMITTEE.
COLLEGE PREACHERS.
PROGRESS OF THE COLLEGE.

Class Histories.

SENIOR CLASS.
SENIOR DIGNITY.
JUNIOR CLASS.
SOPHOMORE CLASS.
FRESHMAN CLASS.
PREPARATORY CLASS.

Associations and Clubs.

THE BATTALION.
GLEE AND BANJO CLUBS.
LIBRARY CLUB.
Y. M. C. A.
Y. W. C. U.
BOTANICAL CLUB.
ZOÖLOGICAL CLUB.
COLLEGE ALUMNI ASSOCIATION.
ANNUAL MILITARY BALL.
CHECKER CLUB.
GOOEY CLUB.
CHEMICAL CLUB.
LIST OF PERIODICALS IN THE READING ROOM.
IN MEMORIAM.

Athletics.

COLLEGE ATHLETIC ASSOCIATION
COLLEGE ATHLETICS
BASE BALL.
FOOTBALL.
LIST OF PLAYERS.
THE TWELFTH OF NOVEMBER.

Literary Department.

THE FALSE ALARM.
A CLASS BASEBALL GAME.
THE CHEMICAL LAB.
THE LIBRARY.
THE SONG OF THE CHEMIST.
THE NEW REGIME
INCIDENTS IN THE CAREER OF A GRIST EDITOR.
THE NEW COURSES
CINCINNATI ORATIONS
THE ECLECTIC SOCIAL
COLLEGE ENTERTAINMENTS.
RECOLLECTIONS OF THE BLIZZARD.
PRIDE GOETH BEFORE A FALL.
COLLEGE ALPHABET.
FEARFUL TO CONTEMPLATE.
CORRESPONDENCE.
RECENT ADDITIONS TO THE LIBRARY.
GENERAL CALENDAR
BITS OF ADVICE.
GRINDS.
JOKELETS.
SCENE, THE DAIRY.
AU REVOIR.

Dedication

TO

Miss Putnam

OUR INSTRUCTOR AND CLASSMATE,

WE,

WHO APPRECIATE HER KINDLY INTEREST

AND PRIZE HER FRIENDSHIP

RESPECTFULLY DEDICATE

THIS VOLUME.

Board of Editors

Editor-in-Chief

ARTHUR E. MUNRO.

Assistant Editors

J. RALEIGH ELDRED.   EDITH GODDARD.

CHARLES N. WHEELER.

Business Manager

HENRY M. BRIGHTMAN.

Introduction.

Merciless Critics:

ONCE more the GRIST appears for your consideration, and ere you bury yourself in its contents we pray you to tarry in your impatience for a little chat with the editors.

In regard to the scope of this Annual we want it distinctly understood that we are in no respect rivals of the College Catalogue. We will try not to bore you with any long prosy sketches regarding early history of the institution, or with any suggestions of the dry unending slavery of the class-room. So we bid you throw away all thoughts of cramming and final exams, and to begin with a free and careless mind the perusal of that true portrayer of college life, its annual.

Many weary months ago five gay, self-confident Juniors met to begin the great task of the year. Since that time they have lost the thoughtless gayety of their merry youth, the heavy load of responsibility upon their shoulders having caused a look of thoughtful gravity to appear upon their once unclouded brows. In the prosecution of their Herculean task they have been supported only by visions of Senior Electives and Snap Courses which will sometime be within their grasp.

Among the serious duties of our positions we have occasionally found stray scraps of humor [?] which we could enjoy if we had the time. Our Board meetings have been the occasion of much controversy, both friendly and otherwise. Vast amounts of sarcasm at different times have been used by some member who has been foiled in some pet measure.

We have duly appreciated our duty in the matter of grinds, and have endeavored to dispose of the question in the most scientific manner. If by roasting one person we could make twenty laugh, we have thought the game worth the whistle and have proceeded to do it thoroughly.

It would amuse you perhaps to suggest that the Grist was a firm opponent of bluffing and a model of veracity. But consider that we have passed the fiery ordeal of the reviewing committee from whose merciless hands nothing escapes, except the barest most literal truth. It was the fear of this ordeal that has filled our minds during the year and restrained our too ambitious pens.

But much suffering reader, do not lose all faith in human nature, there is still some honesty left, for the Grist stands as the exponent of undoubted veracity and the ardent opposer of all forms of bluffing.

We will not make any plaintive boasts as to the hard work that we have done; we have no desire to attract commiseration; it was our business and we did it as best we were able. Several new departures will perhaps be noticed about the Grist in its general appearance and contents. We hope that they will please you, for we have endeavored to publish a book which would at least approach the excellence of former years.

Naturally we would be pleased to receive your approval but will candidly inform you that we will not be annoyed in the least by any darts of criticism which you may possibly hurl at us since we have taken pains to clothe ourselves with the most impenetrable armor. We hope that we have succeeded in breaking the ice, and now invite you to feel perfectly at home in the following pages.

Rhode Island College of Agriculture and Mechanic Arts.

Corporation.

HON. MELVILLE BULL	Newport County
HON. C. H. COGGESHALL	Bristol County
HON. HENRY L. GREENE	Kent County
HON. GARDINER C. SIMS	Providence County
HON. J. V. B. WATSON	Washington County

Officers of the Corporation.

HON. HENRY L. GREENE, *President*, P. O., Riverpoint, R. I.
HON. C. H. COGGESHALL, *Vice-President*, P. O., Bristol, R. I.
HON. GARDINER C. SIMS, *Clerk*, P. O., Providence, R. I.
HON. MELVILLE BULL, *Treasurer*, P. O., Newport, R. I.

BOARD OF MANAGERS.

College Calendar for 1899-1900.

1899.

Fall Term

Aug. 31 and Sept. 1, 10 A. M.	Entrance Examinations.
September 19, 10 A. M.	Exam. of Conditioned Students.
September 18, 19, 10 A. M.	Entrance Examinations.
September 20, 1 P. M.	Term begins.
	Thanksgiving Day.
December 22.	Term ends.

1900.

Winter Term

January 2, 10 A. M.	Exam. of Conditioned Students.
January 2, 1 P. M.	Term begins.
January 25.	Day of Prayer for Colleges.
February 22.	Washington's birthday.
March 30.	Term ends.

Spring Term

April 9, 10 A. M.	Exam. of Conditioned Students.
April 10, 1 P. M.	Term begins.
	Arbor Day.
May 30.	Memorial Day.
June 17.	Baccalaureate Sunday.
June 19.	Commencement.
June 20, 21, 10 A. M.	Entrance Examinations.

Faculty and Assistants

JOHN HOSEA WASHBURN, PH. D.,
PRESIDENT.
Professor of Agricultural Chemistry.

HOMER JAY WHEELER, PH. D.,
Professor of Geology.

*ANNE LUCY BOSWORTH, B. S.,
Professor of Mathematics.

E. JOSEPHINE WATSON, A. M.,
Professor of Languages.

WILLIAM ELISHA DRAKE, B. S.
Professor of Mechanical Engineering.

†OLIVER CHASE WIGGIN, M. D.,
Professor of Comparative Anatomy and Physiology.

WILLIAM WALLACE WOTHERSPOON,
Captain 12th Infantry, U. S. A.,
Professor of Military Science and Tactics.

HARRIET LATHROP MERROW, A. M.,
Professor of Botany.

ARTHUR AMBER BRIGHAM, PH. D.,
Professor of Agriculture.

GEORGE WILTON FIELD, PH. D.,
Professor of Zoology.

FRED WALLACE CARD, M. S.,
Professor of Horticulture.

ADELAIDE SMITH, B. S.,
Acting Professor of Mathematics.

‡JAMES DE LOSS TOWAR, B. S.,
Assistant Professor of Agriculture and in Charge of Civil Engineering

* Absent in Europe for the year.
† Resigned September, 1898.
‡ Resigned May 1, 1898.

JOHN EMERY BUCHER, A. C., Ph. D.,
Associate Professor of Chemistry.

ARTHUR CURTIS SCOTT, B. S.,
Assistant Professor of Physics.

MABEL DEWITT ELDRED, B. S.,
Instructor in Drawing.

MARY WATKINSON ROCKWELL, B. L.,
Instructor in Languages.

LUCY HARRIET PUTNAM,
Instructor in Expression.

THOMAS CARROLL RODMAN,
Instructor in Woodwork.
Appointed, 1890.

HOWLAND BURDICK, B. S.,
Assistant in Agriculture and Farm Superintendent.

HELEN ELIZABETH BROOKS,
Instructor in Stenography and Typewriting.

MARSHALL HENRY TYLER, B. S.,
Master of the Preparatory Department.

JAMES SIDNEY ALLEN, Jr., A. B.
Instructor in History and Political Science.

FRANK EDWIN CRAIG, B. S.,
Instructor in Mechanical Drawing.

GEORGE BURLEIGH KNIGHT,
Assistant in Ironwork.

NATHANIEL HELME,
Meteorologist.

Graduate Assistants

*CHARLES SHERMAN CLARKE, B. S.,
Assistant in Mechanics.

JOHN FRANKLIN KNOWLES, B. S.,
Assistant in Woodwork.

*LOUIS HERBERT MARSLAND, B. S.,
Assistant in Mathematics.

College Activity Committee.

Dr. Field, *Chairman*

B. E. Kenyon, *Secretary*

Members

Dr. G. W. Field	Dr. J. E. Bucher
Mr. M. H. Tyler	Miss E. J. Watson
Miss H. L. Merrow	Miss M. W. Rockwell
B. E. Kenyon, '99	J. J. Fry, '00
C. S. Burgess, '01	R. N. Maxson, '02

College Preachers

Oct. 2, 1898.		S. M. SAYFORD, Newton, Mass.
Oct. 16,	"	REV. MR. GARTH, Wakefield, R. I.
Oct. 30,	"	REV. MR. EDWARDS, Wakefield, R. I.
Nov. 13,	"	R. A. SCHWEGLER, Brown University.
Dec. 11,		MR. HELME, Kingston, R. I.
Jan. 8, 1899.		REV. P. D. ROOT, Wakefield, R. I.
Jan. 15.	"	PROF. C. F. KENT, Brown University.
Jan. 22.		REV. ALEX. MACCALL, Briarcliff Manor, N. Y.
Jan. 29.		MR. M. V. RICE, Providence, R. I.
Feb. 5,		REV. MR. FOBES, Peacedale, R. I.
Feb. 12.		REV. FRANK H. PALMER, Boston, Mass.
Mar. 5.		MR. EUGENE W. LYMAN, Yale Theo. Seminary.
Mar. 12,		MR. H. A. JUMP, Yale Theological Seminary.
Mar. 19,	"	PROF. LORD, R. I. College.
Apr. 9.		PROF. F. H. VERY, Brown University.
Apr. 16,	"	MR. HOLDEN, Attleboro.
Apr. 23,	"	MR. BLANCHARD, Yale Theological Seminary.
Apr. 30,	"	MR. H. A. JUMP, Yale Theological Seminary.

Progress of the College

THE growth of the college this year has been one of steady advancement, unmarked by any particularly striking events.

The long-contemplated new courses were put in operation at the beginning of the fall term. The Freshman class was, as expected, small, but the Preparatory division was gratifyingly large. In scholarship the students have made a better record than ever before. With the Freshmen of next year we hope the college will enter upon an era of large classes.

There have been a number of changes in the Faculty. Miss Bosworth has been pursuing studies in Germany, and her place has been filled by Miss Smith, Wellesley, '90. Mr. M. H. Tyler, Amherst, '97, has been made proctor and instructor in mathematics. Mr. J. S. Allen, Jr., Brown, '98, has been appointed instructor in history and political science. Mr. Frank Craig, Worcester Polytechnic Institute, '98, succeeded Mr. Clark as assistant in mechanics. Mr. Barlow, University of Vermont, and Mr. Marshall, Massachusetts Institute of Technology '97, have been assistants in Dr. Field's department. Mr. Barlow left the college to accept a position in Kansas University. Mr. Card, Cornell, '92, began his work here this year as professor of horticulture.

Since the building of Lippitt Hall, the various departments have enjoyed increased facilities for their work, and that crowded, cramped condition, so well remembered by the older students, is a thing of the past. A new barn has been added to the equipment of the agricultural department, greatly increasing its facilities for instruction, and making it possible to furnish the dairy products necessary at the boarding hall. It is a handsome structure and well adapted for its purpose.

At the beginning of the year a Committee on College Activities, modelled after the now defunct Amherst Senate, was placed in charge of the social and other activities of the student body. It is composed of a Faculty committee and a representative from each of the four classes.

Social life has made considerable progress. The annual Military Ball was managed in a praiseworthy manner by the battalion officers. In the winter term Miss Putnam's Expression classes gave a recital which reflected credit on the students and teacher. The Junior Musicale proved of great benefit to The Grist. The character and success of the entertainment render it a source of pardonable pride to the class of 1900. In the early part of the spring term the Glee Club gave a concert which showed careful training.

The general status of athletic efforts has greatly improved. In the fall term the football team was uniformly successful. More interest and confidence is felt in the Athletic Association than ever before. In baseball, although the material on hand is perhaps not equal to last year's, there is, nevertheless, an evident disposition to work hard for the team.

Some of the old clubs have died a natural death, but the success of the Library Club and Glee Club is encouraging. The two religious societies have been active during the year, and different speakers have delivered addresses at the afternoon chapel services on Sunday.

We are glad to record in The Grist these evidences of prosperity, and hope that they are but forerunners of greater progress in the future.

Scene---The Dairy

Two Men standing in the centre of the room—A group of opossums in one corner—absolutely no other scenery.

One Man—"This *must* stop. I can't enjoy my Sunday evening walk about the grounds with my little friend, because such sounds break the evening stillness in the vicinity of Watson House. I heard from headquarters that this must cease. Let me hear no more of it."

(An opossum comes up and slowly wags his tail, but receives no attention.)

The Other Man—(with show of dignity)—"I, as one of the chief originators of said noise cannot possibly see how it concerns you——"

(Exit Man No. One).

The Other Man—(alone and wringing his hands, from which drops the blood of two hellbenders, three chickens and one hen).

"What shall I do—shall my character be spoiled in the making? Shall I be drawn into it against my will? I will confess all—Nothing will I withhold—It is the only way."

(Exit amid the smiles of the opossums).

The Classes

Senior Class

Officers

B. E. KENYON, President.
   A. W. BOSWORTH, Vice-President.
     M. W. HARVEY, Secretary and Treasurer.

Members

ALFRED WILSON BOSWORTH,	Boston, Mass.
RALPH ORDWAY BROOKS,	Somerville, Mass.
LILLIAN GEORGE,	Amesbury, Mass.
MILDRED WAYNE HARVEY,	Wickford, R. I.
CARROLL KNOWLES,	Kingston, R. I.
HARRY KNOWLES,	Point Judith, R. I.
BLYDON ELLERY KENYON,	Wood River Junction, R. I.
MERRILL AUGUSTUS LADD,	Bay Shore, L. I.
CLIFFORD BREWSTER MORRISON,	Pawtucket, R. I.
WILLIAM FRAZIER OWEN,	Cannonsville, N. Y.
EBENEZER PAYNE,	Lyons Farm, N. J.
WALTER CLARK PHILLIPS,	Wickford, R. I.
ROBERT SPINK REYNOLDS,	Wickford, R. I.
MINNIE ELIZABETH RICE,	Wickford, R. I.
ABBIE GERTRUDE SHERMAN,	Kingston, R. I.
GEORGE ALBERT SHERMAN,	West Kingston, R. I.
SALLY RODMAN THOMPSON,	Wakefield, R. I.

Senior Class History

WHEN the organization now known as the Class of '99 first descended on the venerable quiet of Kingston, few, if any, of its members had the slightest idea as to what would befall them. Our first sensations were those of awe and dread. Every one we met seemed to be a personage of great importance. The disdainful smiles that greeted us from every quarter kept us fully aware of a humiliating fact, our utter insignificance. But in spite of all this our great desire was for knowledge, and the studious life we then led, helped us to forget our youth and unimportance. How far this most laudable desire has been realized we do not care to say, but chapel lectures and other sad experiences have taught some lessons which we expect to retain.

But we manfully conquered our peculiar difficulties, and after we obtained our military suits, we were like all other Freshmen; it would have taken a lengthy fishpole to have reached us. However, our first year was a successful one, for we had athletic victories, and we also built that architectural masterpiece, the old drill shed, which was the forerunner of Lippitt Hall. Just how far this latter building was modelled after the original production of our class, modesty restrains us from telling.

It was one bright September day when we returned as Sophomores, conscious that we had "crossed the awful chasm," to borrow our Milton's phrase. Of course it devolved on '99 to teach the Freshmen a few necessary things, the first of which was physical inspection. Soon after the upper classmen coaxed the "Freshies" into a football game, in which '99 taught them some wholesome, practical lessons. These simple instructions caused our unfortunate pupils to look up to us with considerable awe. In fact the respect for the upper classes was much more apparent then.

than now. We respectfully suggest that a little improvement in this matter would not be out of order. In the winter an epidemic of mumps and measles spread among us, and not a few of our number suffered from the dread diseases. With one more lesson to the Freshmen we ended our second year of college life.

In our Junior year, we held two well-planned receptions, conquered German—more or less—and Calculus. At one time our instructor in German found four modest students in the back row. Their general excellence in class work entitled them to front seats, where they served as examples the remainder of the term. '99 was always said to be a remarkable class in mathematics; no one was surprised at our excellent work in Calculus—a work which was not accomplished, however, without a few slight mistakes. We also published The Grist, which had such unparalleled success that we are thinking of printing a second edition.

Now, we have nearly ended our work here. This last year has been a happy one and we have thoroughly enjoyed it. With '99 at the head of military affairs, all feel that peaceful security which springs from well-grounded confidence. Our mechanical men are prepared to solve any problem in hydraulics, run a blast furnace, or build bridges in the most approved manner. So we feel sure that all the mechanics about the place is well cared for, and that the head of our army has no fear of a loss of the departmental honor or of an embalmed beef scandal.

At last, not without some regret, we bid adieu to The Grist. Our expectations now await Commencement. As we look forward into the future,

> We hear a voice you cannot hear,
> Which says we cannot stay;
> We see a hand you cannot see
> That beckons us away.

Senior Dignity

IT was on the night of the 16th of December. The sweet strains of music were still lingering in the ears of the students, as they made their way from Lippitt Hall to their rooms. Occasionally an air from one of the selections just played would float upon their ears as it was whistled by some musical genius and the Juniors were congratulating themselves upon the unparalleled success of the evening's performance. Except for the occasional boiler explosion, fire alarm, or the croak of a Freshman, there was naught to disturb the blissful reveries which all were enjoying. Even Tip Tyler was visiting Jim Allen instead of making his customary rounds of inspection.

Suddenly the walls begin to shake and tremble. Book racks tumble, picture frames rattle, and the whole atmosphere is convulsed by a noise, such that the roar of cannon, the echos of Ladd's voice when heard in the reading room, or even the chatter of Eldred's teeth when the Dr. called him into the office, are not to be compared with it. Those who are brave enough, cautiously look out of their doors to ascertain, if possible, the cause. But the everwatchful Tip only knows that it is an unlawful racket, and that it is his duty to stop it at once. He therefore launches forth on a tour of investigation, and locating the scene of action in room 32, makes his way there P. D. Q.* Thrusting open the door, his astonished gaze meets the cause of the great upheaval of forces. Two grave and reverend brethren of '99, not satisfied with the entertainment of the evening, are adding a sequel. At the farther end of the room, the brother from Point Judith is acting the part of the Prima Donna of the evening, while the brother from Pawtucket is pacing ceaselsssly back and forth, each step of his iron heel shaking the building anew, and presenting the singer with

---
*That is, with great alacrity.

bouquets innumerable. At first, a frown of disgust settles on the features of the proctor, then, as he takes in the humor of the situation, it changes into a smile such as only he can give. He pushes into the room, grasps a frightened *Senior* in either hand, and gently leading them toward the door, remarks in his persuasive voice,

"COME BOYS, YOU HAD BETTER GO TO YOUR ROOM."

"·Go·to·your·rooms."

Junior Class

LUCY HARRIET PUTNAM, our long suffering honorary member. We call upon her whenever we are in need, or discouraged, or in debt, and she proves a valuable friend by scolding, exhorting or encouraging, as the case demands. She has a great fondness for Boston, and leaves us without any warning at the most unaccountable times. Boston is an attractive place.

Lucy Harriet Putnam.

Edith Goddard.

EDITH GODDARD is a cheerful jollier from the word go. She is the great authority in the English class, where she delivers with great volubility crammed Chaucerian phrases and scraps of old mythology. Her social progress during the past two terms has been most marked, especially manifested by the number of her evening "At Homes."

ROWENA HOXIE STEERE is a young lady with a very independent spirit As witness, her cuts in Trig, and other cuts which she has distributed with no less unsparing hand. She has always been a day student and a resident of Alton.

BERTHA DOUGLAS TUCKER is a typical conservative, with a mint of lofty ambition. She takes pride in her class standing, although she strikes something occasionally in which she does not capture an A. A great stickler for class honor and dignity.

MORTON ROBINSON CROSS. This slim youth is a professional photographer. Formerly a leader in athletics, he has retired from active service this year. When he weighs one hundred and sixty pounds he expects to pitch for Yale. This is his last year at Kingston, but we bow to the inevitable, for we have been aware that he was staying here only to get his growth.

Roena Hoxie Steere.

ELIZABETH MAY PARKHURST is a young lady whom Wickford is proud to claim. She is an expert stenographer and a great lover of one hour per day courses. Although she has her share of college pat-

Bertha Douglas Tucker.

riotism, we fear that other institutions claim part of her allegiance.

RALPH NELSON SOULE, our great athlete. On the ball field no one has more "push" and "pull" than he. For years he has been in training, not only in the gymnasium, but also in matters of diet. He eats a plenteous supply of crackers and milk, when they are to be had, and at other times meat. His recipe for becoming stalwart is based upon the principle that eating fat meat makes one fat, therefore eating tough meat makes one tough.

Morton Robinson Cross.

JOSEPH ROBERT WILSON is a good, all-round fellow, who never makes a fuss. There is but one dreadful lack in his

Elizabeth May Parkhurst.

character and that is, that he doesn't care for girls. This is deplorable, but we hope that this vacancy will be well filled some day. There is hope, for he is still young.

JOHN RALEIGH ELDRED, is a jack at all trades. He has considerable artistic ability, is musical in every way, playing all manner of instruments and singing all the popular songs. His great and inordinate love for Chapel is very marked, since he is always the first one in his seat every morning. His motto is—"Better late than never." On the athletic field he is unequalled in speed and he catches every ball he touches. I may just mention the fact in passing, as of no importance, that he is a fine student.

Ralph Nelson Soule.

Joseph Robert Wilson.

ANTHONY ENOCH STEERE is a man of promise. For some unknown and unknowable reason, he has learned all his lessons for two weeks; even to his German. You can't "rattle" him in the English class. He can unravel the knotty intricacies in the family connections of those confusing English kings and queens, without a mistake.

ROBERT JOSEPH SHERMAN, familiarly known as "Ancient," is the most venerable personage in our collection of geniuses. His most ardent passion lies in the pursuit of game and fish, in the capture of which he is an expert. Equally famed as a "crowder," he amuses himself and destroys the comfort of others by an extremely energetic use of his violin. He threatens us with his departure at the end of this year, a loss which we could hardly endure.

John Raleigh Eldred.

Anthony Enoch Steere.

AMOS LANGWORTHY KENYON is a substantial individual with pessimistic tendencies. He is the lone star of the Agricultural Course among the naughty naughts and a specialist in the French and German languages. He never makes himself unduly prominent and never runs for office, two extremely good qualities.

LEVI EUGENE WIGHTMAN is one of the most original characters Scituated among us. It is a most amusing sight to see him whip a certain new course "Freshie" into line, a recreation which he especially enjoys. This spring he has worked hard to become a crack base-ball fiend, which one would naturally think a "Swinch," since he is cracked in several other respects. His is a most supple wit, capable of great elasticity.

Robert Joseph Sherman

Amos Langworthy Kenyon.

CHARLES CLARK CROSS is a youth who is amply endowed with several qualities popularly supposed to be monopolized by his Satanic Majesty. We can guarantee that he will never become crazy, since his remedy for all mathematical difficulties lies in "rationalization." This year actuated by some freakish impulse he has abandoned the companionship of the residents of the dormitory for the wilds of West Kingston. In regard to his future we venture to predict that he will never fail for lack of energy.

Levi Eugene Wightman.

Charles Clark Cross.

CHARLES NOYES WHEELER is a faddist of the most pronounced type. He wanders through his courses in a most remarkable manner, always menacing the study committee with the assertion that he will take Stenography and Typewriting if he has to give up everything else. He always take the lectures in advanced physics, which naturally are the most important parts of the course. "Charlie" has aspirations in the chemical line, where we hope he will find something to satisfy his affinities.

Charles Noyes Wheeler.

Leroy Weston Knowles.

LEROY WESTON KNOWLES is a nondescript character in whose classification one could not venture any farther than genus homo, order Cumana. Beyond that only a few isolated facts can be brought to light. Last year he made a position back of the line on the football team. Rumors were spread about at the beginning of the term that he was a candidate for second base. At this the other candidates all gave up the ghost, and since we could not play a one man team, the management reluctantly gave him notice to retire.

HENRY MAXON BRIGHTMAN is a chap with the most marked commercial instincts. Those who have heard him discourse with great gusto upon the merits of the Regal Shoe, will never question his business proclivities. He has had a

Henry Maxon Brightman.

Ruth Hortense James.

big opening for such talents as he might possess in managing The Grist this year. Being mechanical, he spends much time in that department, where he "astonishes the natives."

RUTH HORTENSE JAMES is a Junior with much latent talent for the study of medicine. She is an adept upon all heart diseases, having made many interesting and successful experiments in that line. She also finds botany interesting as having relationship to the study of medicine. Trig has no charms for her.

Arthur Earle Munroe.   John James Fry.

ARTHUR EARLE MUNROE is the prosperous, strong man of our class. Bicycling, especially upon the Sabbath, seems to agree with him. His favorite ride is along the H—— road, which is always lined with roses without thorns.

JOHN JAMES FRY hails from East Greenwich to whose peaceful haunts he occasionally retires for rest and recreation. "Jack" has always been prominent in athletics and at present holds the captaincy of the foot-ball team. He has distinguished himself this year as class president and as a member of the C. A. C. All things considered he is a most reputable member of the class, barring a few little "pet hobbies" in which he indulges occasionally. On account of excessive diffidence Mr. Fry declines to allow his likeness to be exposed to the vulgar gaze of the public.

LENORA ESTELLE STILLMAN is pre-eminently, first, last and all the time an unremitting grind. One would expect the sudden collapse of the Universe if she should come into the Calculus with her problems undone. She especially abhors all attempts to "try for speed." Truly a prodigy for learning.

Sophomore Class

Officers.

A. A. DENICO, PRESIDENT.
C. S. BURGESS, VICE-PRESIDENT.
H. D. SMITH, TREASURER.
A. B. SHERMAN, SECRETARY.

Honorary Member.

MISS ROCKWELL.

Members.

CARLTON GARFIELD ANDREWS,	Potter Hill, R. I.
NELLIE ALBERTINE BRIGGS,	Shannock, R. I.
CHARLES STUART BURGESS,	Providence, R. I.
LOUIS GEORGE KARL CLARNER, JR.,	Pawtucket, R. I.
EDNA ETHEL DAWLEY,	Kenyon, R. I.
WILLIAM JAMES DAWLEY,	Kenyon, R. I.
ROBERT ELISHA GRINNELL,	Middletown, R. I.
ARTHUR ALBERTUS DENICO,	Narragansett Pier, R. I.
LOUIS JOHN REUTER,	Westerly, R. I.
ANNA BROWN SHERMAN,	Kingston, R. I.
ARTHUR ALMY SHERMAN,	Portsmouth, R. I.
ELIZABETH AGNES SHERMAN,	Kingston, R. I.
HOWARD DEXTER SMITH,	North Scituate, R. I.
GEORGE CANNING SOULE,	Wickford, R. I.
FANNIE ESTHER STILLMAN,	Charlestown, R. I.

Sophomore History.

ONE year has passed since we first met you in the '99 Grist. Our class has lost several members, and among them we especially mourn the absence of "Dingleberry" and "Mascot."

One day early in the Fall term we met for the first time, as Sophomores, to select those who were to be our guiding stars throughout the trials and tribulations of Sophomore life. We elected the following:

For President we chose Denico, a man noted for speed on a wheel, especially when going towards Wakefield. He hails from the Pier. Next we chose a Vice President, Burgess, who is noted in athletics; and whereas he carried sweaters last fall, he is now Captain of our college "Nine." He comes from Providence and is generally known as "Crook." We then elected our Scituate Smith to care for the Treasury and keep the Vice President straight. He is very fond of study. Out of the many Shermans in our class we selected one from Kingston, near "Chickenville," for our recorder of events; recognizing in her ability as typewriter the essential qualities of a Secretary.

The class had very good health throughout the year, owing to the work of Prof. Scott. Contrary to the wishes of some o the class he persisted in giving us "Physics" throughout the year, four times a week. During the winter term he also gave us "Shocks," but in spite of this rough treatment some are even now contemplating the continuance of the course another year.

In the Spring term we commenced Chemistry with Dr. Bucher, but at present have shown no very decided Chemical affinities, although Miss A. B. Sherman and Miss Briggs were told that H_2O consisted of gases, yet when they tried to light it under the Hood it would not burn.

But they are beginners in Chemistry and should not be censured since Munro, who is considered one of the smartest Juniors, did the same thing in his third year. Miss E. A. Sherman says the H2S generators under the Hood are active. Another member of the class, wishing to determine the odor of Cl. heated some conc. HCL in an open dish on his desk. He now knows the odor and the reason that Dr. Bucher cautioned the class to work under the Hood. The aforementioned chemist's name is Andrews.

That we are a very intelligent class is shown by the fact that the entire class was excused from Ex. in English and French in the Fall term ; we have reason to be proud of our athletic record for we have always had men on the college ball teams ; the Glee Club, which was formed for the first time this year, has found our services invaluable.

Remarkably little trouble has been caused this year by members of the two new classes, but the thanks should go to Mr. Tyler, who has taught them their place in College life.

We have had many trials during the year, but we remember that, " All's well that ends well," and will now bid you good-bye till we meet you as Juniors in the '01 Grist.

OFF ON A BAT.

Class of 1902.

LATHAM CLARK
BAILEY JORDAN CORNELL
OLIVER N. FERRY
CHARLES FRANKLIN KENYON
BERTHA MAY BRAYTON

RALPH NELSON MAXSON
JOHN GARFIELD MORTON
ROBERT W. PITKIN
ARTHUR LEONE REYNOLDS

Honorary Member

MISS E. J. WATSON.

B. J. CORNELL, *President.*   O. N. FERRY, *Vice-President.*
A. L. REYNOLDS, *Secretary and Treasurer.*

CLASS YELL: We have none, we say nothing and saw wood.

THIS class entered the College under very different conditions from former Freshman classes. Owing to the new course of study adopted last year, the entrance examinations were much harder than previous Freshmen had to pass and the course of study for the Freshmen this year is fully as hard as that of the Sophomores. This is the reason for the small size of our class, it being the smallest in the College.

After examinations were over and schedules arranged we settled down to hard work, which did not give us much time in which to be homesick. The class was organized in due time and all was well until the Junior Reception. The speech which our class president made on that occasion will long be remembered by him if not by others. He would liked to have published it, but the managers of the Grist could not give us more than ten pages for it, and rather than have it condensed we decided to leave it out altogether.

One surprising thing about our first term here was that none of us got a ducking. From the talk of the older students, we would not have been surprised at any time to have received an exhibition of college spirit in the shape of a shower-bath, but for some reason we did not even get sprinkled. Perhaps the fatherly watchfulness of our genial proctor dampened their spirits and so kept our skins dry.

Of all our studies the first term, probably no recitations were enjoyed as much as those in Physiography. Dr. Washburn always had some interesting story to illustrate the matter we were studying, and we all were sorry when the course was finished.

Some amusing things were apt to happen in Physics, too. One day, the most sedate member of the class became "vicious" and the same day another described how to separate a crystalloid from a "celluloid". Such little things, however, are an interesting diversion, for recitations become dull when everyone knows his lesson well.

As a class we have a pretty good record, but we all have our failings. Ferry is liable to be out at all times of night, sometimes getting in just in time for breakfast; "Doc." goes on a "toot" every drill day and we are not able to stop him; Reynolds is always short and shows no signs of improving; "Max" was unused to restraint, so he moved; Kenyon never says anything so he keeps out of trouble, but Pitkin, although you may not have thought so, is always light-headed and Cornell and Morton have been known to go calling *in the middle of the week*. Morton, by the way, is a special, who got side-tracked here the first part of the winter term and has been taken care of by the Freshmen ever since.

The first secretary we elected had more trouble than a married man. You see his watch stopped and he could not record the minutes as was his duty. A meeting was called to decide whether to give him a new watch to go by or to give him the "go by". As there were but thirteen cents in the treasury we voted that it would be unlucky to buy a new watch.

Max has been acting strangely, he has all his notes type-written. No one knew that Max did that kind of work before, but he has been seen a number of times recently with a new '99 model type-writer of the most approved type. His case will be investigated and reported on later.

The winter term is now over and we are beginning to think of warmer weather and outdoor sports. May we all experience more sunshine, physically and mentally, next term than we did last, and finish our year as well as we started it.

Q. E. D.

A FRIEND IN NEED.

The chairman stood at the desk,
The notices to read,
And as he calmly surveyed the room,
This is what he said,

"The Juniors may come at two o'clock,
The Sophomores at three;
But the insignificant little Preps,
We do not care to see."

Preparatory Class

Officers.

JOHN A. CLARNER, President.
LAURA M. COOKE, Vice President.
KATE G. BARBER, Secretary.
ELVERTON J. CRANDALL, Treasurer.

Honorary Member.

EDNA M. CARGILL, . Abbott Run, R. I.

Members.

WILLIAM H. ALDRO,	Rocky Brook, R. I.
KATE G. BARBER,	Carolina, R. I.
LOUIS F. BELL,	Wakefield, R. I.
THOMAS BRENNAN,	Peacedale, R. I.
HORTENSE B. CARPENTER,	Kingston, R. I.
EMORY P. CHACE,	Warren, R. I.
ALBERT S. CHURCH,	Narragansett Pier, R. I.
JOHN A. CLARNER,	Pawtucket, R. I.
LAURA M. COOKE,	Peacedale, R. I.
WILLIAM J. CONWAY,	Narragansett Pier, R. I.
ELVERTON J. CRANDALL,	Adamsville, R. I.
FREDERICK L. CROSS,	Narragansett Pier, R. I.
JOHN G. CROSS,	Narragansett Pier, R. I.
ROBERT K. DANIELS	Glastonbury, Conn.
J. EDWARD DUFFY,	Riverpoint, R. I.
CALEB G. FLAGG,	Kingston, R. I.
LEIGH GARDINER,	Peacedale, R. I.

Fred C. Hoxsie,	Woodville, R. I.
Willard M. Hoxsie,	Quonochontaug, R. I.
Helen W. M. James,	Kenyon, R. I.
Laura A. Jillson,	Woonsocket, R. I.
Edith Keefer,	Oceanus, N. Y.
Raymond W. Kent,	Woonsocket, R. I.
Garabed Krekorian,	Harpoot, Turkey.
William Loomis,	Glastonbury, Conn.
Harold McFarland,	Sakonnet Point, R. I.
Robert B. McKnight,	Adamsville, R. I.
John H. Mowry,	Woonsocket, R. I.
Milton C. Pascoe,	Easton, Pa.
Arthur N. Peckham,	Kingston, R. I.
George M. Pearce,	Wakefield, R. I.
Mary S. Quinn,	Wakefield R. I.
George H. Rice,	Wickford, R. I.
Edith S. Rodman,	Kingston, R. I.
Albert A. Saunders,	Carolina, R. I.
Emma C. Tillinghast,	Slocumville, R. I.
Leroy Thompson,	Narragansett Pier, R. I.
Everett E. Wheeler,	Shannock, R. I.
Thomas P. Wells,	Kingston, R. I.

Class of 1903.

COLOR—White and Brown.
YELL—Brown and White, White and Brown,
1903 Are Never Down!

ON the twenty-third of September, in the year of our Lord eighteen hundred and ninety-eight, witnessed at "Ye College" at Kingston, a most extraordinary gathering of would be students, known as the "Preps." Yes, we are the survivors of that original congregation, and although we have not much of a history thus far, we have demonstrated our ability, by being the first class to arrange and successfully carry out a "sleigh ride." Although much was done by some of the older classes to prevent our going we finally started out, rather late, but returned safe and sound, being kindly cared for by our ever-ready Proctor, who had a vigilant eye upon his little lambs.

We have not participated in athletics to any great extent thus far, although we contributed somewhat to the success of the foot-ball team last season, but hope to be more successful in the future. As for our studies, it can be said we have done comparatively good work, considering we have been pressed rather hard.

But to leave such mundane affairs and come to our subject, "The Immortals." We have several Jacks at all trades among us. We have a "Barber," who, although not a professional, has done some very good work, considering it had to be "Chace'd" after. Another good point about our class is that we are never in want of food, having on hand at least a "Peck" of "ham" and Mortons of "Rice" than we "Con-way," also being constantly supplied by the "Gardiner," with whom the "Tillinghast" to go on indefinitely, and the product is finally prepared by our "Cooke."

We are, however, misled in the anticipation of our dinner by the sound of a "Bell," which "Pierces" our ears, coming from the "Church" with the two "Crosses," lately constructed by our "Carpenter." But we shoulder our disappointment as we are very good soldiers, and return to our study room with our "Flagg" flying, where the hum of our voices is to the tutor as the click of the "Loom-is" to the practiced weaver, and resume our labors, which we hope are not in vain, but will bring us on an even standing, if not on a higher one than some of our predecessors. Well, I think I have told you everything worth mentioning this year, but as we advance, I suppose we shall encounter many experiences, and next year, when we appear as Freshmen, as we hope to do, we will "Duf-fy" anyone to give a more complete and interesting account of their previous year's work than we of our coming Freshman year.

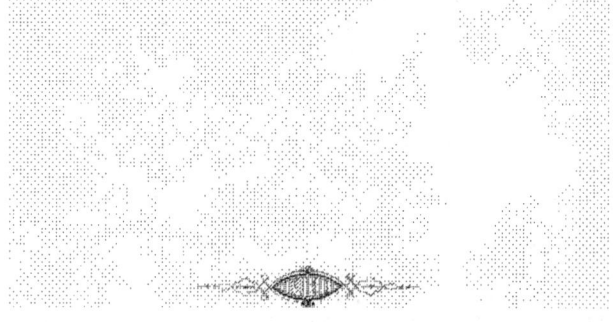

Associations
and
Clubs

Battalions

Military Organization, Rhode Island Cadets

Company A

B. E. KENYON,	Captain.
W. F. OWENS,	Second Lieutenant.
W. C. PHILLIPS,	1st Sergeant.
J. J. FRY,	2nd Sergeant.
A. E. MUNRO,	3d Sergeant.
M. R. CROSS,	4th Sergeant.
J. R. ELDRED,	5th Sergeant.
H. M. BRIGHTMAN,	1st Corporal.
H. D. SMITH,	2d Corporal.
A. L. KENYON,	3d Corporal.
A. A. SHERMAN,	4th Corporal.

Company B

M. A. LADD,	Captain.
A. W. BOSWORTH,	First Lieutenant.
H. KNOWLES,	1st Sergeant.
R. N. SOULE,	2d Sergeant.
C. KNOWLES,	3d Sergeant.
C. N. WHEELER,	4th Sergeant.
A. A. DENICO,	5th Sergeant.
C. S. BURGESS,	1st Corporal.
A. E. STEERE,	2d Corporal.
L. G. K CLARNER,	3d Corporal.
L. E. WIGHTMAN,	4th Corporal.
2d LIEUT. W. F. OWENS,	Adjutant.
C. N. WHEELER,	Sergeant Major.
L. CLARK,	Bugler.

BATTALION DRILL.

Rhode Island College Glee and Banjo Club

Officers.

C. B. MORRISON, '99, PRESIDENT.
R. O. BROOKS, '99, BUSINESS MANAGER.
C. S. BURGESS, '01, TREASURER.
J. S. ALLEN, JR., DIRECTOR.

Glee Club:

First Tenors.	Second Tenors.	First Bass.
C. S. BURGESS, '01.	R. O. BROOKS, '99.	L. J. REUTER, 01.
J. S. ALLEN, JR.,	C. B. MORRISON, '99	J. A. CLARNER, '03.
R. N. MAXSON, '02.		W. M. HOXIE, 03.

Second Bass.

L. G. K. CLARNER, '01.   C. G. ANDREWS, '01.
A. W. BOSWORTH, '99   J. E. DUFFY, '03.

Banjo Club:

Banjeaurine.
A. C. SCOTT.

Mandolin.
C. B. MORRISON, '99.

Banjos.
C. G. ANDREWS, '01.
J. A. CLARNER. '03.

Violin.
L. G. K. CLARNER. '01.

Guitar
J. S. ALLEN, JR.

GLEE AND BANJO CLUB.

The Library Club.

THIS club was organized at the beginning of the college year, to fill the place formerly occupied by the old Research Club. It enjoys a reputation for exclusiveness, since its membership is mainly recruited from the higher classes and the faculty. The method of work taken up by the members consists in a systematic review of the leading magazines and periodicals, together with a review of the most prominent books as they appear from the press. Different magazines are assigned to the several members who, at the semi-monthly meetings give a synopsis of their contents and a detailed review of the more salient articles. During the year the club has held meetings regurlarly, which have been conducted with much pleasure and profit to the members. Its career on the whole has been very successful and we join with the members in crying, " Long live the Library Club."

Y. M. C. A.

W. M. HOXIE,	PRESIDENT.
H. D. SMITH,	VICE-PRESIDENT
R. W. PITKIN,	{ COR. SECRETARY. { REC. SECRETARY.
A. L. KENYON,	TREASURER.

Y. W. C. U.

M. W. HARVEY,	PRESIDENT.
B. E. BENTLEY,	VICE-PRESIDENT.
E. M. PARKHURST,	SECRETARY.
E. P. WELLS,	TREASURER.

Alumni Association

HOWLAND BURDICK, PRESIDENT.

GEORGE A. RODMAN, SECRETARY.
Woonsocket, R. I.

LOUIS H. MARSLAND, TREASURER,
Franklin, N. Y.

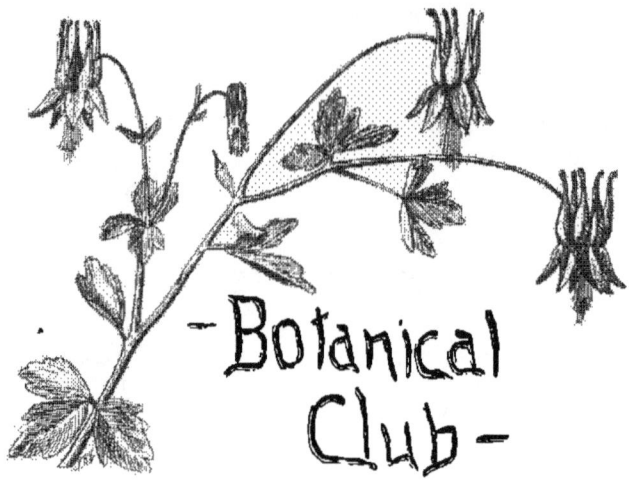

Botanical Club

In Charge of the Professor of Botany.

Those interested in botanical subjects meet occasionally to discuss the local flora and simple botanical literature.

Zoological Club

The Zoölogical Club meets bi-weekly for the study of the local fauna, for the presentation of brief papers, and for the review of current journals. A special room is devoted to the collections and preparations made by the club. The daily observations by the members upon the occurrence, habitat, structure, life history and habits of the animals are on file for ready reference. Special excursions are made to favorable localities. Opportunities for field work in zoölogy are remarkably fine.

Officers

C. B. MORRISON,	*President.*
H. KNOWLES,	*Secretary.*
E. PAYNE,	*Curator.*

Officers

L. E. WIGHTMAN, President.

J. J. FRY, Vice-President.

C. F. KENYON, Secretary and Treasurer.

Winner of Tournament

C. F. KENYON.

Gooey Club

Officers

LYMAN CRANSTON,
Guard High Custodian of the Sacred Goo.

R. NELSON MAXSON,
Most Indefatigable Hitter of the Pipe.

ARTHUR L. REYNOLDS,
Assidious Devotee of My Lady Nicotine.

R. N. SOULE,
Defender of the Royal Meerschaum.

HOWLAND BURDICK,
Humble Worshipper of the T. D.

Recollections of the Blizzard

THE heavy snow storm of Sunday and Monday, February twelve and thirteenth completely demoralized passenger traffic on the various railroads. Consequently a number of the students who went home on the Friday night before the storm found it impossible to return to the College before Wednesday morning. One young man we have in mind, on entering the reading room for the first time after his return, looked around him for a moment like some one just awaked from a long period of dormancy and asked in a stentorian voice: "Does any one know what day it is, or what time it is, or anything about the time whatever? I have lost track of everything relating to time during this storm."

Now every one knows that all conversation must cease upon entering the reading room, and a look of intense surprise immediately showed itself upon the faces of those who happened to be present at that time. The librarian looked at the offender with one inquiring glance, which gradually changed to a curious smile.

The young man did not ask any more questions regarding his locality or the time of day, so it was assumed by those present that he had found a suitable answer for one or both of his questions.

List of Periodicals to be Found in the Library

- Harper's Monthly.
- Atlantic.
- Century.
- Scribner.
- Cosmopolitan.
- N. E. Magazine.
- Popular Science Monthly.
- Chautauquan Monthly.
- American Naturalist.
- Engineering Magazine.
- Manufacturer and Builder.
- North American Review.
- Forum.
- University Magazine.
- Quarterly Review.
- Westminster Review.
- Educational Review.
- School Review.
- Art Amateur.
- N. E. Journal of Education.
- Blacksmith and Wheelwright.
- Carpentry and Building.
- Review of Reviews.
- American Journal of Science.
- Astronomy and Astrophysics.
- Journal of Franklin Institute.
- Power.
- Botanical Gazette.
- Bulletin of the Torry Bot. Club.
- Journal of Society of Chemical Industry.
- Public Opinion.
- Harper's Bazaar.
- Harper's Weekly.
- London News Reprint.
- Life.
- Puck.
- Judge.
- American Machinist.
- Electric Age.
- Electrical World.
- Engineer.
- Engineering.
- Scientific American and Supplement.
- New York Critic.
- Forest and Stream.
- Breeder's Gazette.
- Quarterly Journal of Economics.
- Political Science Quarterly.
- Journal of Chemical Society.
- University Extension.

National Geographic Magazine.
Popular Astronomy.
American Mathematical Monthly.
Science.
MacMillan Magazine (Nature).
New York Daily Tribune.
Boston Daily Herald.
Washington Daily Post.
The American Kitchen Magazine.
The Journal of School Geography.
Boston Cooking School Magazine.
Journal of the U. S. Artillery.
Journal of Military Service Institution.
The Brochure Series
Forest Leaves.
Florist's Exchange.
American Gardening.
National Nurseryman.
Canadian Horticulturist.
Gardening.

IN MEMORIAM

PETER BRADY

DIED AUGUST 6, 1898

IN MEMORIAM

ARNOLD THEODORE GRANT

CLASS OF 1900

DIED 1898

IN MEMORIAM

NELLIE HOLLIS PIERCE

CLASS OF 1899

DIED 1898

IN MEMORIAM

IN MEMORY OF
WILLIAM HENRY ALBRO
DIED MAY 6, 1899

WHEREAS, It has been the will of the Almighty in His infinite wisdom, to remove from our midst our beloved friend and classmate, William Henry Albro, and

WHEREAS, We recognize his scholarly attributes, his friendly, generous spirit, and his sterling character, therefore be it

Resolved: That we, the members of the Preparatory Class of the Rhode Island College of Agriculture and Mechanics Arts, keenly feeling the loss of so worthy a member, do extend our heartfelt sympathy to the bereaved family in their affliction, and be it further

Resolved: That a copy of these resolutions be sent to the family of our departed classmate, and that copies be placed on file in the Class Records and be published in the college and other publications.

E. M. CARGILL,
J. E. DUFFY,
H. J. CRANDALL,
For the Class.

DISTORTED FEATURES A SPECIALTY.
(Taken by Camera Club.)

Athletics

College Athletic Association

Officers

WALTER C. PHILLIPS, President.
WILLIAM F. OWEN, Vice-President.
JOHN J. FRY, Secretary.
CLIFFORD B. MORRISON, Treasurer.
MARSHALL H. TYLER, Auditor.

College Athletics

THE Athletic Department of any college is necessarily one which requires much conscientious labor and sacrifice to make it a success; and if properly conducted it cannot fail to be the institution's greatest pride and glory. In these modern days intellectual life and grade of scholarship are not the only things taken into consideration by a young man about to enter college, and undecided where he will enter; he also studies the athletic records of the different institutions, and is most apt to select one which is prominent on the baseball and football fields. It may confidently be asserted that the college which does not use every effort to promote its athletics has fallen short of its highest usefulness as an educational factor. The responsibility rests alike upon faculty and student body, which should co-operate in the work of placing good teams in the field to compete with neighboring institutions. To attain this result, it is necessary that the students give the Association not only financial aid, but a hearty sympathy and support, which will work wonders.

One of the best signs of athletic activity is a large number of candidates for the different teams. Every position should be competed for by several men, thus insuring a strong team and securing good material for future use. Oftentimes an excellent player is found where one would little expect it. This condition also tends to develop a greater number of the students, which is preferable to the production of a few prize athletes.

While a healthy spirit of rivalry is greatly to be desired, still the competing schools should be careful that no bad feeling is created. A spirit of jealousy and spite between two schools defeats the object of athletics and causes many incidents which are afterwards looked upon with regret.

The attainment of success necessitates hard work and much sacrifice, but it cannot fail to bring good results ; and if continued, will sooner or later place athletics upon a firm basis.

Chemical Club

Artful appropriator of abstractable apparatus,	ANDREWS
Perpetual producer of phenomenal precipitates, .	. MORRISON
Calamitous creator of coliquative concoctions,	. CROSS
Earnest eliminator of excessive exertion,	ELDRED
Fallible filterer of formidable fluids, .	. FRY
Sloppy shaker of slimy solutions. . , . .	. STEERE
Investigator as to the nature of the tri-nitro-hydroxy-oxy benzoic pyrogallic diphenyl aldehyde, .	. MORRISON
Synthetic investigator of rubber, .	. BROOKS

Chemical Apparatus

Retort (Large).	BOSWORTH
Blowpipe, .	. L. CLARKE
Gas generator,	WIGHTMAN
Night-ric acid.	. OWEN

Base Ball.

THIS sport has, ever since the earlier days of the College, been the object of much interest, and a pardonable pride has been taken in the efforts of the team.

Last season our nine was peculiarly successful, winning six out of eight well-fought games. This team, in its individual makeup and team work, was the best nine that has ever represented the College on the diamond during previous years.

At the beginning of the season less than half of the old team were in College, and upon these as a nucleus the present team is built. A goodly number of candidates have competed for the various positions and by the regular practice it is hoped the team will make a creditable record for itself.

The schedule as given below contains seven games, the first of which was a walkover for the College.

Games Scheduled

April 22.	R. I. C. vs. Bulkeley H. S.,	30— 5
April 29.	R. I. C. vs. Rogers H. S., 6 innings,	6— 2
May 6.	R. I. C. vs. E. G. A., 10 innings,	7— 6
May 13.	R. I. C. vs. W. A. A.,	1—13
May 20.	R. I. C. vs. Storrs College,	Cancelled.
May 27.	R. I. C. vs. Friends School.	
June 3.	R. I. C. vs. Storrs College.	
May 27.	R. I. C. vs. Friends School,	
June 3.	R. I. C. vs. Storrs.	

Base Ball

C. B MORRISON,   MANAGER.

VARSITY NINE.

C. S. BURGESS (Capt.)	Third Base.
A. A. DENICO,	Pitcher.
C. C. CROSS,	First Base.
J. J. FRY,	Second Base.
W. F. OWEN,	Catcher.
R. S. REYNOLDS,	Short Stop
W. C. PHILLIPS,	Left Field.
J. E. DUFFY,	Center Field.
L. F BELL.	Right Field

Substitutes.

A. E. MUNRO.   R. B. MACKNIGHT,

L. E WIGHTMAN.

BASE BALL TEAM.

Football

THE football season of the fall of '98 gave great encouragement to those interested in college athletics. A schedule of five games was played without a defeat. Our record was one which we are proud of and in after years we shall look back upon it with pleasure.

This year's team has an advantage which previous teams have always lacked—good, continious coaching. Mr. Marshall Tyler, Amherst, '97, began his services as one of the college corps of instructors this year, and it was owing to his interest and efficient coaching that the success of our team was made possible.

At the beginning of the season only three of the '97 team were in college. Owing to this state of affairs it was necessary to develop players from new material. From what at the beginning seemed a hopeless task great success was attained, a team being developed which was worthy of the college. This making of a good team from a list of candidates consisting almost entirely of new men, was one of the most encouraging features of the season.

Throughout the season the regular team practiced against a strong second one. This was the best possible training and also the means of bringing good substitutes to the front.

The great interest of the student body and faculty was shown by a large attendance at the games and by good financial support.

FOOT BALL TEAM.

Football

C. B. MORRISON, MANAGER.

W. F. OWEN (Capt.)	Full Back.
J. J. FRY,	Right Half.
L. W. KNOWLES,	Left Half.
R. N. SOULE,	Quarter Back.
C. C. CROSS,	Right End.
J. EMMETT,	Right Tackle.
A. A. SHERMAN,	Right Guard.
R. B. MACKNIGHT,	Centre.
R. E. GRINNELL,	Left Guard.
W. M. HOXIE,	Left Tackle.
R. O. BROOKS,	Left End.

Substitutes.

F. HOXIE,	A. E. STEERE,
A. A. DENICO,	L. J. REUTER,
R. N. MAXSON,	C. S. BURGESS.

Games Played

Oct. 7.	R. I. C. vs. W. H. S.,	12 to 6
Oct. 15.	R. I. C. vs. W. A. A.,	33 to 0
Oct 29.	R. I. C. vs. Providence High,	16 to 0
Nov. 5.	R. I. C. vs. Brown, '02,	5 to 0
Nov. 12.	R. I. C. vs. E. G. A..	20 to 2

The following review of the individual players will possibly be of interest to the reader,

Capt. Owen, '99, at fullback was the backbone of the team. He was a reliable line bucker, the man for the position.

Sherman, '01, at right guard was a strong player, especially good in defense.

Emmet, '00, at right tackle was an old veteran. His weight and knowledge of the game made the team strong at this point.

Cross, '00, at right end was a good ground gainer and sure tackler.

MacKnight, '03 for a new man was a sturdy centre, who throughout played an honest, aggressive game.

Grinnell, '01, left guard, was a strong player.

Hoxie, '03, left tackle, was the strongest man in the line, and sure of good gains when given the ball.

Brooks, '99, played a clean game at right end.

Soule, '00, at quarterback was an acquisition. He combined good passing with clever headwork.

Fry, '00, right halfback, was a good runner, quick to notice an opening in the opponents' line.

Knowles, '00, was a good gainer on end plays in his position as left halfback.

As substitutes, Reuter, '01, Burgess, '01, and Steere, '00, were on hand as backs, while F. Hoxie, '03, Denico, '01 and Maxson, '02, were held for use in the line.

On the whole the condition of athletics shows a very creditable advance over the preceding seasons and a considerable rise in school spirit.

Literary Department

The False Alarm

The gloomy robe of night had covered College Hill,
All were in bed and everything was still,
And when the watchman had finished quite his round
The silence was complete, one could not hear a sound.

Hardly had he touched the pillow, hardly closed his eyes in sleep
When the bell began its ringing, sounded at his very feet.
Up he started in a frenzy, throwing coat and sweater on
Not stopping for revolver, in a second he was gone.

Scarcely had he reached the landing, where was standing A. E. Steere,
Shouting with great vigor, something loud, distinct, and clear;
"Oh, Col. Ben. Bosworth come out of your room below
And conduct us to the danger, we're in readiness to go."

The Kerosenes struck a match, Becky and Ladd and Ben,
Who went hunting to find his "six choice men."
While he went upon his search with authoritative ire,
A sound breaks out upon his ears, the sudden call of fire.

Then Owen, always at duty, to the pump house ran in haste,
And as soon as he entered, doctored the fire with waste.
Morrison in a fine frenzy rushed to the room of Prof. Jim,
Stood there vigorously pounding, and shouting into the darkness dim.

The Sophs ran to the hose cart, but knowing not where to go,
Until the "Watson House" was cried by those who always know.
When the cart was rushed over the frozen ground,
While to the different buildings the students thronged around.

"Regal's" quick inspection produced evidence enough
To show the impatient waiters the depth of the wily bluff,
Then dispersing quickly, back to their rooms they go,
Each inquiring of the other the things they want to know.

When the fun was over the proctor did appear,
And make a hasty census, to find out who was here.
The message was sent to the pump house over the electric wire,
Which conveyed with undue warmth the absence of any fire.

Much discussion there has been as to the sudden cause
Of this great upheaval of physics' unerring laws.
" 'Tis relays, crossed wires, fire drill," say some,
And theories pile up mountain high, ad infinitum.

Proverbs.

Spare the crib and spoil the exams.
A Prep and his hair are soon parted.
Cut your recitations to fit the position you hold in the estimation of the faculty.
A ball in the hand is worth two in the air.
There's many a slip 'twixt entrance and graduation.
Don't brag of your marks till you get your report.
A hit in time saves the nine.

The Twelfth of November

IT was a glorious day, for it marked the victorious close of the most successful football season of the Rhode Island College. On this date was played with the East Greenwich Academy the game which was of greatest interest to the students. Although in strength their team was not to be compared with the Brown Freshies and Providence High whom we had previously vanquished, still, owing to the old-time rivalry between the College and the Prep. School it was regarded as the most important game of the season.

The weather was of the typical football variety, clear, cool and bracing, with hardly any wind to interfere with the game. In the morning the team, accompanied by a large following of enthusiastic rooters, left the College for the Academy. On the way down much noisy enthusiasm was evident, showing itself by oft-repeated college cries.

When the Kingston boys reached the town, they broke up into small parties, some inspecting the Academy and its surroundings, others walking through the streets impatiently awaiting the time of the game.

Finally the hour for the line-up arrived, and the two teams ran out on the field loudly cheered by their respective supporters. The college team made a fine showing with their new suits and a full complement of substitutes. The rooters for each faction had chosen opposite sides of the field, waiting to encourage their players at every gain made. The female portion of the Academy contingent was very noticeable with its gay red flags, which before the game had progressed far, drooped in a most remarkable manner.

It is unnecessary to describe at length the game, which throughout was an encouragement to the Kingston students and a reward for constant systematic practice. The ball was in the hands of the college men most of the time and they made good use of it. With irresistible dash, the backs plunged through the opposing lines, making substantial gains every time the ball was put in play. The college boys encouraged by the enthusiastic cheering of their delighted supporters, rushed the ball across the line for twenty points during the game and at the close the ball was in dangerous proximity to the opponents' line, where a good play would have quickly scored another touchdown.

At one time only did the Academy boys offer any effective opposition to the visitors. This was in the second half when they braced up and carried the ball the length of the field, where it was lost on downs. However the college was forced to make a safety, thus giving the Academy players their two points.

The college girls, who had started for the Academy in a large barge were tardy and witnessed only the latter half of the game.

On the way home a more noisy and excited crowd could be seldom found. The welkin rang with cheer after cheer for the team, for the members who had distinguished themselves, and for our coach, whose perseverance and hard work had made this victory possible.

Such was the end of the season in which we had won five successive victories, not marred by a single defeat. We had put forth the best team of recent years, encouraged hard competition in athletics, and we hope stimulated a more healthy school spirit and love of one's college which after all is the true end and aim of all inter-scholastic athletic efforts.

The Last Game

THE campus of one of our New England colleges was dotted with several groups of students, among which were two groups of five each who were representatives of the Sophomore and Freshman classes. These students were attracting considerable attention from the others who were present, because they were making the final arrangements for the game of base ball which was to be played on the following afternoon between the Sophomore and Freshmen classes, and which was to be the last game of the season. Both teams had practiced incessantly for this event and the rivalry between them was of the keenest. Each team was sure of winning the game; so whenever a Soph would meet a Freshman, an exciting argument was the result. This it was that caused such a large congregation of students on the campus on that particular afternoon. The conversation was finally brought to a close as the Sophs turned to go away, saying, "To-morrow we will show up your team by not letting them score one run." " We will see about that," answered a Freshman, while each crowd moved off in a different direction.

While the Freshmen were sure of winning, still they were afraid that their pitcher, who had been hit by a batted ball at a practice game a week before, would not be able to play the whole game. "If he should be compelled to give up before the end," thought they, "our chances of winning will be very small." He had told the captain that he did not feel the effects of his injury, but the captain's face wore a doubtful look.

Belonging to the Freshman class were several young men who seemed never to take any interest in athletics of any kind. They were always to be seen with books in their hands, and apparently cared for nothing but study. One of these was Bert Waters and another George Simmons. They of course had not tried for positions on the class team because they could not spare the time for practice. But they were fond of base ball just the same; and as Bert had been the pitcher for the S——'s before coming to college, he and George would play together for a few minutes each day, unknown to the other members of their class. In a short time Bert had become quite expert at "twirling" and George equally expert at catching.

The next day was an ideal one for base ball, and nothing was talked about but the game in the afternoon. It was scheduled to begin at 2 o'clock sharp, and by 1:30 the grand stand and the bleachers were well filled with people from the neighborhood. It was exactly 1:50 when the Sophomore team marched on to the field led by their mascot. A mighty cheer arose from the enthusiastic spectators, which was repeated five minutes later as the Freshman team appeared. A few moments of practice by each team showed that they were in prime condition.

The Sophs won the toss and the Freshmen took their places in the field. "All ready! Play Ball!" shouted the umpire, and the great game commenced. The Freshman pitcher gave the first man his base on balls which brought forth a cheer from the Sophomores who occupied the benches quite close to the team "Oh, he's easy" they shouted; "we won't do a thing to him." The next two men were struck out, which caused the Freshmen on the opposite side of the field to give three hearty cheers for their pitcher. The next man hit the ball and reached first base in safety, while the man who was there ran to second. The next man struck out and the Sophomores took the field. The Freshmen did not score, although one man reached third base. The next three innings were played without a score being made by either side. But the Sophs came in from the field at the beginning of the fifth inning with a determined look on their faces, showing that they were determined to make a score. They had noticed in the last inning that the Freshman pitcher was giving out. This encouraged them. The first man was struck out, but the second made a hit. The Sophomores yelled themselves hoarse. But when the next batter sent the ball over the center fielder's head, and never stopped running until he reached third base while the man on second base ran home, the crowd went nearly wild with enthusiasm, and shouted and cheered as only an enthusiastic crowd can cheer. But the Sophs were more determined than ever. They pounded the ball all over the field and retired at the end of the inning with a score of five runs to their credit.

The face of the Freshman pitcher was now a ghastly white. He told the captain that he had wrenched his arm that was injured a week ago, and could not pitch any more. The game was not delayed, as the Freshmen were at the bat, but the captain thought it would be almost impossible for him to find another pitcher in time for the next inning. He went over to where the crowd of Freshmen were sitting on the bleachers, and inquired if any of them could take the injured pitcher's place. "Of course the game is lost," he continued, "but the Sophs will make no end of sport of us if we do not finish it."

A moment of profound silence.

Then Bert Waters stepped out from among the seats and said in a firm voice, "I will try it you will let me."

"You," laughed the captain, "what can you do? I don't believe you ever saw a base-ball."

"But I have, and I know how to pitch one, too," replied Bert, and his look of confidence was having its effect on the captain.

"Well, you may try it," said the captain, wondering if he were in a dream.

"But I must have my catcher, as we understand each other," said Bert, as the captain started back toward the diamond.

After few moments of discussion, Bert was told to go the dressing-room, where they would find suits, get into them, and appear on the field as quickly as possible. When the regular catcher heard of this he was very angry and said that he hoped the Freshmen would not score one run.

In a few minutes Bert Waters and George Simmons appeared in uniforms, and many remarks were made about them, such as "What are those fellows going to do? How did they learn to play ball? by studying a Greek grammar?" But the new players paid little or no attention to these wild remarks, as they took their positions on the field. The Sophomores were in high spirits. They thought of the honor and fame that this victory would give them. The Freshman captain had lost all hope of winning the game, but was anxious to score at least one run to keep the team from being whitewashed.

At the beginning of the sixth inning the score stood 5 to 0 in favor of the Sophomore team, and Bert occupied the pitcher's box while George was behind the bat. The first Soph to bat made a two-base hit which was cheered by the crowd. The next man advanced him to third on a sacrifice, but he did not reach home because the next two men were struck out, which retired the side. The Freshmen came to bat and scored two runs, which caused an enormous amount of cheering by the Freshmen on the bleachers. The Sophs came to bat and the first three men were struck out in one, two, three, order, and the Freshmen began to have a faint hope of winning or at least tying the score. They came in from the field and scored three runs before they were put out, thus tying the score. The eighth inning neither side scored. The Sophs now came up for the last time. The first man made a three-base hit. The second was struck out. The third hit the ball and it went up in the air. The catcher started after it and caught it with one hand about half way between the home plate and third base, and touched the man who had started to run home from third, thus making a double play and preventing the Sophs. from scoring. If the Freshmen now could only make one run the game would be theirs. The first man up was struck out. The second made a two-base hit and the excitement of the spectators was intense. They cheered every time a ball was thrown. The next man was put out at first base. It was Bert's turn at the bat and he trembled somewhat as he picked up his bat. The ball went whizzing past his head. "One strike," called out the umpire. The next two balls went wide and of course were called balls. The next one was a good one and Bert struck with all his might. He hit the ball squarely and it sailed into the air. It went straight over the right fielder's head and Bert made a home run. The man on second also ran home, making a total of 7 to 5 in favor of the Freshmen.

The game was over and the Freshmen were happy. Bert was the hero of the hour. Everyone was eager to shake hands with him, and it was twenty minutes later when he was picked up by four stout Freshmen and carried on their shoulders to the dressing room, while four more followed with his friend George, the catcher.

The Sophomores could not be found. They had gone to their rooms to look up their Greek and Latin grammars to see if they could find anything about base-ball. It is not known whether they found anything relating to that sport or not, because they never mentioned base-ball again that year.

The Chemical Lab

NO one who has not studied Chemistry, can understand the mysteries of the Chemical Lab. Its long low roof covers dark facts and the genius who dwells there forcibly tears secrets from Dame Nature, harnesses up that poor lady's resources and uses them for his own ends. The odors which eternally float about the roof of the building, like those same clouds which are said persistently to stick to the top of Mt. Blanc, make one snuff curiously in passing. Let this article be for those who don't understand these things. Of course, all that I can say won't, *can't* present the real thing but can give only a slight, fleeting glimpse of that sacred precinct.

When we're new to that science, we have more formality in the class room. We assemble in the lecture room and are counted and lectured at. Dr. B.—does almost all of the experiments at first, by way of teaching us care and precision. We yearn for the time to come when we can explode our own hydrogen, boil our own acids and break our own test tubes. Later in the Qualitative Course, we go directly to our own street and number, unlock our door and immediately set up housekeeping. The desks are very well equipped and it does'nt take long to find out the use and (ab) use of every article of furniture. This is the merry water bottle which will keep up our spirits through many a weary filtering. It's interesting, too, to see how far a stream of water can be made to go when necessary. What is pleasanter than to pour a tiny stream of H_2O upon the top of an unsuspectinghead, intent upon discovering whether the H_2S has been expelled. The start of surprise as the said person discovers that he has water on the brain, is equally pleasing. Then again, for variety, turn out the faithful gas, which is trying to evaporate to dryness some sort of juice, and let your neighbor wonder a bit.

The great social center is the middle hood. There everyone gathers to filter, wash, talk, and endure odors. There is absolutely nothing to do for a few minutes, while the filter is going through but be conversational. I've heard most heated theological discussions under the hood, heard someone make a proposal, heard presented questions of ethics and food. Nothing is too trivial to discuss over the heads of the H_2S generators and the acid bottles. I may not close without saying a few words about the Marsh Test. Be firm with it and it won't explode. Don't let your nervous sphere communicate itself to the generator and all will be well. The hydrogen will do right, if you wait long enough.

If Chemistry appeals to you at all, you will find those afternoons in the Lab. very interesting and pleasant, and I wish you all success with the "unknowns."

The Library

THE Library is a most popular resort. If you wish to forget heart troubles, ulcerated teeth, conditions, hunger or physics just throw yourself upon a book and kindly oblivion will surround you. There are rows upon rows of tranquil books ready with a hearty welcome. The very atmosphere of them is restful. They never thrust themselves upon you nor ever chide you, but are extremely frank and friendly. If you have a mood, then match your mood to a book and be at rest. Here we travel, history, fiction,—anything you like. Or nibble here and there : this book is brutally frank; that, courteous; this, scientific; that, jolly.

It is a most satisfactory sight to see the room filled with lines of heads, of all colors and all degrees of dishevelment, buried to their neckties in books. Woe to the person socially inclined, for the kindly dragon never sleeps. It is one of the best things in the world that we do have to "restrain our skipping spirits," in this place at least. Otherwise how could one learn a whole week's history or botany in five minutes, if surrounded by whispered scraps about the last dance or the latest hat ? Impossible ! Nothing ever disturbs us more, save the wild scream of the escaping steam in the engine room, or the audible smile of a Puck or Judge reader.

The Library has grown. Once it had only wall shelves and a stray case or two in the middle of the room. Now the book stacks almost crowd us out, and they did crowd out the stately palm which grew, or rather refused to grow, in the intellectual sphere of the place. Perched upon the stacks are Morrill, our benefactor, and Sappho. They never look at each other; yet it would be so interesting for two such bright people, so differently brought up, to fathom each other's mind and be sociable.

I must say a few words about our illustrious Library Club, which meets twice a month. The monthly periodicals and some of the other recent publications are reviewed in turn. No one would imagine from the calm appearance of M - x - - n when giving a synopsis of Scribner's, that a wild and hurried half hour had just been passed, before the opening of the Club, in trying to cram all the ideas in that magazine into his head. New members keep coming in; and as soon as their names are proposed, they are set to reviewing a four-volume work which is just out, or a scientific article. That's a good way to do, for then one's turn comes less frequently and the new members gain a good understanding of said book. The new members, too, not being initiated, study their articles thoroughly and well. Growth is a glorious thing.

And now it is time to close the Library and lock the door for the night. Let the souls of the books come out and converse. Methinks one can hear, as one passes down the hall, the ghostly laughter of Shakespeare and Chaucer as they look at Life, or catch the wild whispers of Dante and Milton intent on a picture representing the infernal regions, in the latest Puck; and then all is silence.

LIPPITT HALL.

The New Regime

SUCH is the title that the average student felt disposed to give to the new order of things which has been in force during the year. How well we remember the day when Prexy, with suitable emphasis, disclosed the details of his plan for the administration of the dormitory. We were promised proctor with a monopoly on all the virtues possessed by the ideal ruler. He was to arrive at the beginning of the year with a carpet bag full of rules calculated to strike the meek submissive Prep with terror, and to quail even the boisterous gayety of the hilarious Soph. Remembering the free and easy character of the former military rule, our busy minds ever prone to contrast, were filled with terrible visions of disciplinary severities and punishments. Nor were our apprehensions removed by our first glimpse of the new incumbent. His athletic stature and impressive mien inspired one with a belief that offences against that hypothetical carpet bag of regulations would not be tolerated and that perhaps punishment would be meted out with no unsparing hand. Such was the impression, and the effect was salutary to the authorities. Pranks were at a discount, securities on tricks quickly fell below par, and a quietus was put on all forms of hazing Thus we dwelt in peace and security, would be offenders were kept in check by that omnipotent fear of the all-pervading arm of the law. The Fall Term passed and yet the studied quiet was not broken. But let us not be deceived. 'tis but a silence that portends a more lively turn of affairs.

It is the Winter Term, the Chicken Class and many other kindred evils are upon us. With great perseverance our worthy protector had inculcated into our moral system a due sense of the new responsibilities which had devolved upon us as a direct consequence of the visitation of Providence with which we were afflicted. Strict silence was enjoyed upon us during the dreary watches of the night. Under the shadow of these solemn fear inspiring edicts, we lived in a trembling state of apprehension. About this time, a statement was made in Chapel, which in the light of later events was doubtless rather premature. Certain remarks were made in a jocular manner of the deep laid plans of some scheming students in regard to ejecting certain mighty men of muscle through the window on some eve. After this students with whom you and I are acquainted could be detected trying to control their goats and at the same time racking their brains to invent some wily scheme for the edification of friends. The result of all of this cunning scheming is too well known to be dwelt upon by this my humble pen. Well we all remember the sudden occurrence of certain local showers which owed their origin to an innocently deceptive can, perched over doors of unsuspecting students. But the final results of these erratic meteorological phenomina were tragic as is shown by the career of a prominent specialist of purifaction.

All can recall that evening when our proctor proved recreant to his duties and upon his return found his ingress suddenly blocked. By use of Herculean strength the opposing chair was quickly reduced to smithereens. With the cunning of "Old Sleuth" the clues were investigated with true detective skill. But all in vain the culprit remained undiscovered, free to continue his career of intrigue. Are you sure?

Such is the result of obedience to false gods and such is the condition of affairs in our hitherto peaceful haven of rest. But do not suppose my gentle reader, for an instant, that all this was allowed to pass unnoticed for in justice there was found a remedy for all these ills. Banishments were decreed and certain of our students in their search for higher things were suddenly removed to a much lower plane where it was supposed they could with greater profit continue their school career.

But let us stop here, our reluctant pen is loth to chronicle these melancholy events. Our pensive hearts throb with sorrow as we survey the few remaining vestiges of our former priviliges No more the peaceful quiet inviting the reflective youth to studious retirement, to undisturbed revery and meditation. In their place is stealth and intrigue, the constant strife of warring factions and the indiscriminate attentions of the practical joker. But much is Fate, we bow in submission to the powers that be, and murmur, not our will but thine be done.

The Song of the Chemist

(With apologies to Tennyson).

Break, break, break,
  The beakers and test-tubes, Oh, see!
And I would that I might utter
  The thoughts that arise in me.

Here comes the watchful Professor,
  With an unknown solution for me;
And I would that I might know
  What the metals in it be.

He tells me to lower the window,
  And to keep my work under the hood;
For the smell of chlorine and H_2S,
  To the nostrils is not good.

Filter and wash the precipitate,
  And dissolve in HCl,
(Oh, that all this Chemistry
  Could be transferred to —— Cairo.)

Break, break, break!
  Beakers and test-tubes so free.
May recollections of my chemistry course
  Never come back to me.

Eclectic Social

THE Eclectic Society is a thing of the past. Its members parted without a qualm for its funds provided each one of them with a ticket, which fact fulfilled all their expectations. The memory of the last social, is also passing away from us. Before it is quite erased from our minds, let me recall it.

Behold a group of students, anxious to please and eager to make the affair a success. There are games of one kind and another and refreshments of like description. There is a noise, some laughter, and here are the Seniors, suave, hair neatly combed and well blacked shoes. They bring cheer and joy while their unwonted gentlemantly attention and thoughtfulness quite astonish the committee.

For some unknown reason, the refreshments all disappear during the first half hour—entirely gone; for some few with studied carelessness, quietly but earnestly gathered about the lemonade bowl like birds of prey around some choice morsel. It was discovered later that the bowl was quite dry. We play a game entitled "Advice". It is very wholesome for Fate holds the pack and deals out the cards with unerring wisdom. After some more games and music, the party begins to break up. Then with civil leers and graceful flops these same guests passed out with that uplifted smile which is seen but once in a lifetime.

And the next morning when the young ladies swept the Chapel and cleared up generally, the kindly sphere of brotherly love was so all pervading in the Chapel that it had to be swept up into dustpans and removed to prevent suffocation.

Bits of Advice

"All meals will be served in the air, as no dishes will be allowed on the table." *Percy.*

"Guests wishing to take a bath will find it convenient to use soap and water." *Mowry.*

"No one will be allowed to sleep after retiring." *Chase.*

"The 'glee club' will sing after the students retire." *Allen.*

"Those wishing to visit "Wolf Rocks" can do so by returning the sign 'Wolf Rocks 200 Yds.'" *Munroe.*

"Persons wishing exercise are recommended to drill." *Col. Ben.*

"Persons sitting on the front porch will find it agreeable to hold an umbrella over their heads." *Clarner.*

"Students depositing valuables in the college safe, will do so at the owner's risk." *E. M. Cargill.*

"Extra charges will be made for the use of the electric lights after half past ten." *A. C. Scott.*

No charges will be made for the gym lockers. Keys furnished at the store at 50 cents each. *A. C. Scott*

College Entertainments

IN recalling some of the events of college life during the past year, it is encouraging to note an effort on the part of the students to provide entertainments of literary or musical interest and a tendency to depend less as an attraction upon the excellent facilities for dancing afforded by Lippitt Hall. It is especially pleasant for the Juniors to be able to claim the first, and not the least successful, of the year's courses, which occurred on December sixteenth.

Junior Musicale

In arranging this, the first purely musical affair given at the college, the class was fortunate enough to secure a string orchestra comprising several well-known Providence musicians. These were assisted at the piano by Mr. Joseph Hastings, Jr., whose musical abilty and wide experience were potent factors in the artistic success of the concert, and also by the solo numbers of Miss Annie E. Rider, soprano, and Mr. Andrew Ford, violinist. To the musical program was added, very appropriately, a reading by the honorary member of the class, Miss Putnam.

The excellent work of the orchestra and soloists met with hearty appreciation throughout, especial enthusiasm being shown for Mr. Ford's brilliant playing of the Hungarian Fantasia, the reading given with such strong dramatic effect by Miss Putnam, and the song from Ambroise Thomas' *Mignon*. Among the numbers most enjoyed were also two not on the program; for before Miss Putnam was permitted to leave the stage, she had quite captivated the house by her reading of the amusing verses "In May," recited with piano accompaniment; while Miss Rider responded to the applause which greeted *Mignon's* pathetic song, with a translation of the little German poem, "Liebstraum," set to music by Mr. Hastings. The beautiful Pilgrim's Chorus died away into a moment of silence, which was perhaps more eloquent than the round of applause that followed, and the lights went out that night on some very well-contented Juniors, whose pleasure was in no wise lessened by the fact that the affair had proved a substantial benefit to The Grist.

In leaving the subject of the Musicale, we are glad of the opportunity to express the gratitude of the class to those who aided in its success: to Miss Rider, Miss Putnam and Mr. Hastings, to Mr. Sidney S. Rider for programs; to Miss Eldred for posters; and to all the Faculty for their encouragement and support.

Recital by Pupils in Expression.

On January twenty-eighth, a very pleasant recital was given by several of Miss Putnam's pupils, assisted by Miss Mary Belle Smith, violinist. The readings were all very successful, and bore witness to Miss Putnam's thorough and able training, as well as to the inspiration which she has been to her pupils in their work. Equally creditable were the tableaux, so artistically devised and skilfully carried through. The varying effects of colored lights made them most interesting; and the last, "Rock of Ages," was strikingly effective, the most beautiful of all in the graceful lines afforded by the grouping of the figures. A welcome addition to the program was the playing of Miss Smith, already well known to college audiences.

Glee Club Concert

One of the most gratifying events of the year was the first concert, on April twenty-first, of the College Glee and Banjo Club, organized under the direction of Mr. Allen. It has long been the wish of those interested in college affairs, that a greater interest in musical matters might be aroused in the students, and that such talent as existed among them might be developed and made a more prominent factor in the pleasures of college life. The advent of a leader able to bring order out of the musical chaos, was therefore felt to be a matter for rejoicing; and the results of the winter's work, as shown at the concert, fully justified the hopes of those interested in the experiment. The singing of the Glee Club revealed some excellent voices, in a state of training remarkable for so recent an organization; while the playing of the Banjo Club was hardly less admirable. They were assisted by Miss Thompson.

The work of the Glee Club was especially satisfactory throughout, notably in "Kentucky Babe," with its humming refrain over the odd and very effective suggestion of a banjo accompaniment, and in the Eton Boating song, where it was supplemented by the Banjo Club. The solos gave an encouraging indication of the possibilities of college talent; and the Quartet was very well received, both its selections being encored, as were several numbers by the Glee and Banjo Clubs. The encores added an acceptable dash of spice to the program, as they were all very well given, decidedly amusing and extremely brief. Miss Thompson's readings gave much pleasure, especially the chapter from "the Birds' Christmas Carol," also her encore number, a quaint little poem by James Whitcomb Riley. The concert was an unqualified success, and reflects great credit upon the faithful work of the Club, and on the able leadership of Mr. Allen. It is sincerely hoped that another year will show the progress justly expected from so auspicious a beginning.

"Pride Cometh Before Destruction"

Sunday, 19th, - - - - - - .

It is such a pleasant day, sunny and wide, it is large enough for me with my new military suit on. I think I'll go to the station and see the newcomers, maybe there'll be some girls. Come on, " Rastus."

Out they start and as they proceed their spirits rise in (inverse) proportion to their common sense.

Do any of my readers know the brook between the College and the station? It is a very naughty brook. Just at the point, where there ought to be a bridge, but isn't, there are merely some slippery logs. BEWARE! Over goes No. 1, in his beautiful, shiny, spotless suit, hat-leaving curls and turning and twisting in varying currents as it seeks a more congenial spot. People are known by the company they keep, friend No. 2, and over he goes. Water drowns their—what was that bubbling up through the stones? — not an oath surely !

Just then Fate in the shape of a small, yellow bird perches upon a twig o'erhead and sings, " Oh ! where are my wandering boys to-night ? " And the waters of the night moan wildly over the two black stones.

The New Courses

In 1897 the standard of the College was raised and new courses of study were outlined to take effect in the fall of '98. This was done in conformity with the recommendations of the report adopted by the Association of College Presidents at a meeting held in Washington, D. C., in Nov. 1896.

The necessity of having the degree given by the different state institutions represent approximately the same amount of work was the cause of the action; this tends to produce a uniformity in their several courses of instruction.

Since, however, this change in admission requirements would necessarily exclude many country pupils, who have not had the advantages of High School instruction, it was thought best to conduct a preparatory department in connection with the College. The examinations for admission to the preparatory school are the same as as those formerly required of Freshman.

At the beginning of the Sophomore year the number is enlarged by the separation of the Mechanical from the Physical Mathematical. In the last two years the Chemical course stands alone.

Later, a General Course will be added to the curriculum to benefit those who wish to enjoy the advantages of instruction without being obliged to take any technical work.

A conspicuous fact noticeable in the new courses is that they mean hard work. The former strategic evading of conditions is now much more difficult to accomplish successfully.

Much regret is sometimes expressed by the upper classman that these courses were not in force when they entered.

With the above mentioned hard work and a high quality of instruction, we venture to predict that in a few years a degree from the R. I. C. will give the holder a feeling of pardonable pride and a consciousness that its value is appreciated by the educational world.

Incidents in the Career of a Grist Editor

IT would be too much to expect that the career of so unimportant a personage as "Ye Grist Editor" would possess any interest to the casual reader. Nevertheless our minds would rest easier if we could unburden some of our troubles to the possibly sympathizing reader.

Let no one think for an instant that the scribe lives in an atmosphere of constant pleasure, rejoicing in the use of an impliment, popularly supposed to be more powerful than the sword. On the contrary his days are days of toil and trouble ever searching grinds on some poor chap. Even in his slumbers he is not allowed to rest unmolested, he is haunted in his dreams by the ever present name of "Grist" and he imagines himself the recipient of summary vengeance from the unfortunate under graduate whom he has roasted.

Of course the editor is ever pursued by the honeyed attention of some student who is anxious to escape for one year the roasting from the annual. One of our friends in an outspoken way stated that he did not want his name used as he wanted to take a copy home with him.

There is always the person who thinks that he has an especially bright idea which he is firmly persuaded should find a place in print.

As a consequence one is confronted with some threadbare witticism and the suggestion "Put it in the Grist," "Put it in the Grist " How often some student has come to us, his form doubled up in a fit of convulsive laughter, to relate some ancient joke long ago worthy of a decent interment, while with the tears streaming down his cheeks he would utter the words, "Put it in the Grist," "Put it in the Grist."

General Calendar

1898.
Sept. 21. College opens.
  22. Course of study committee doesn't want anything to do with the Preps.
  23. Doc. receives great applause after his debut as a bugler.
  28. Saunders breaks his arm. Exhibition fire drill.
  29. Some revelations at Athletic Association meeting.
  30. Fire at Chickenville.
Oct. 7. Junior reception. Football game, R. I. C. vs. W. H. S.
  9. Kent sees something exciting.
  12. A lecture by Professor Brightman attended by all the literati and lovers of music. Rastus is assassinated.
  14. Immense inundation of individual invitations which emanate from the Watson House. Several "dicers"
  15. Football game, R. I. C. vs. Wakefield A. A.
  17. Denico walks up from the depot this morning.
  29. Football game. R. I. C. vs. Providence H. S. Initial straw-ride of the season.
Nov. 1. Great football enthusiasm shown after the announcement by the management.
  2. Steere proves the following law: "If infinity were here there could be no parallel lines."
  5. R. I. C. beats Brown Freshies. Great celebration in the evening, concluded by liquid refresments at the Watson House.
  7. Great fire at the Boarding Hall. Burnt the beef-steak.
  10. The apostles of Physiography attend ye Mechanic's Fair in a body. Si. gets lost and walks all the way home from Boston.
  12. Football. R. I. C. vs. E. G. A.
  18. Saunders cuts gymnasium.
  20. Mac and Rastus fall in the brook.
  22. A little tonsorial work performed in room 16 about midnight.

	30.	Bozzie has a runaway.
Dec.	5.	The barber is blackballed.
	5.	Lucky bag is opened.
	8.	Crandall has a smashup.
	9-16.	Several Seniors try to start poster collections.
	15.	MacKnight gives a vivid representation of Macbeth.
	16.	Junior Musicale.
Jan.	3.	Winter term opens.
	6.	New spirit infused into drill through the influence of Prexy.
		Pitkin strays into conic-sections recitations and doesn't know where he is at.
	11.	Gorilla appears in chapel with his hair curled.
	20.	Military Ball. Influx of never graduates.
	28.	Recital by expression classes.
	29.	Great religious piety as shown by open air praise service in the vicinity of the Watson House.
Feb.	13.	Ice. Great absence of Juniors from recitations.
	3.	Miss W - - - - n dismisses a class ten minutes early. Eldred and Cornell work at the machine shop till eighteen minutes past four.
	4.	Chickens depart.
	5.	Moving day in dormitory. Payne invited to secure lodgings elsewhere.
	8.	Several signs appear in Lippitt Hall which arouse Scott's ire.
	10.	Prep. sleigh ride. 10° below zero.
	16.	Meeting of Board of Editors.
	21.	Washington's birthday hop. Miss P - t - - m receives a box of choice cut glass flowers.
	22.	The Faculty continue the festivities of last night.
Mar.	1.	Feminine inspection of dormitory. Extreme disgust on the part of A. L. K. and others.
	3.	Eldred went to chapel.
	16.	Chase takes a private lesson in drill.
Apr.	22.	Baseball season opens with a victory. R. I. C., 30; Bulkeley, 5.
May	3.	All the young ladies are requested to meet in the gymnasium. As a consequence, a large section of plastering falls from the ceiling below.

College Alphabet

A is Andrews, an amiable Soph,
   His smile is warranted not to wear off.
B is for Bosworth, the world-renowned colonel,
   You may read of his exploits each day in the Journal.
C is Cornell, a jolly good fellow,
   He wears a shirt of most beautiful yellow.
D stands for Denico of athletic fame,
   Who walked up from the station the day after the game.
E is for Eldred, who all may see,
   Is a model of punctuality.
F is for Faculty, who grind out the marks,
   And condition all students who are too fond of larks.
G is for Grinnell, whose delicate frame,
   Knocked dear Mr. Sibley 'most out of the game.
H is for Henry who works night and day,
   Concocting great schemes to make The Grist pay.
I —but here we are interrupted by a voice which cries in tones of authority, "I am M - - - - -l A - - - - - - s L - - d, who command Company B, and strike terror to the hearts of all who come under my iron sway at the dining hall. There are no other I's worth mentioning, so don't try." We obey silently and pass on to,
J meaning Jays too numerous to mention,
   In various ways they compel our attention.
K is for Kenyon, active enough
   In enforcing the rules of the Physic's Prof.
L denotes Love, a Senior elective,
   Which knocks other studies quite out of perspective.
M is for Maxson, fiend from the West,
   Society former and lover of rest.

N is for Newton whose loss premature,
   With resignation we strive to endure.
O —Owen, the depth of whose fascinations
   Far exceeds that of his recitations.
P must be Pascoe, an infant in size,
   But whose mischief and impudence rise to the skies.
Q is for Queer things, each class has its share,
   But the Preps can lead all the rest, for fair.
R is for Reynolds whose somnolent tendency,
   On most occasions obtains the ascendency.
S stands for Stillman and also for Steere,
   To whom Analytics is quite without fear.*
T is for Thompson, whom I won't describe here,
   You can read about her in The Grist of last year.
U is for Uncle who left his old lair,
   To pursue his agricultural study elsewhere.
V is for Vineyard, that little collection,
   Whose charms the day students know to perfection.
W —Wilson, Wilby, Wheeler, now whom
   Shall I choose, but, alas! I've used up my room.
X ams and Xcuses Xpose our slim knowledge
   Of the arts and the sciences taught in the college.
Y is for yells whose importance is great
   In foot-ball games and all matters of state.
Z is for Zero; one is nothing alone,
   But two denote something whose worth is well known.
& highly we prize it, don't blame us we beg,
   For surely there's naught like the double goose-egg.

---

*For different reasons, however.

Recent Additions to our College Library

551
MP 356. B. J. Cornel.
    THE ART OF PUBLIC SPEAKING.

644
J 346. R J. Sherman.
    ADVENTURES OF A HUNTER.

363
K 71. M. A. Ladd.
    TREATISE ON THE FIST PERSON SINGULAR.

9685
DZ 7Q L. W. Knowles.
    PRACTICAL BUMMING, or HOW TO BE A SPORT ON SMALL MEANS.

285
KS V46. R. N. Maxson.
    COMPENDIUM OF BRIGHT AND WITTY SAYINGS.

83
GY 257. L. E. Wightman.
    FARTHEST UP.

41144
PDQ. C. C. Cross.
    THE MANY WAYS OF DOING IT. HOW TO PASS EXAMS.

6482
WKX 71. C. B. Morrison.
    THE PERFECTION OF THE ART OF BLUFFING.

GFK. A. C. Scott, B. S.
　　MONOPOLIES, THEIR BENEFITS AND ADVANTAGES.

9563
MV 168. M. H. Tyler,
　　THE CARE OF CHILDREN.

9851
ZW. A. E. Munroe,
　　HOW TO WIGGLE CHAIRS.

The following communications which the Grist Board has at different times received are here printed for the benefit of the reading public who will without doubt peruse them with great interest:

Editors of The Grist,

DEAR SIRS:—

I direct this letter to you, asking a favor which you cannot consistently deny one with such lofty pretensions as myself. I am, to tell the truth, not averse to notoriety, and would be pleased if you devote some space to the consideration of a few of my many achievements. Possibly you know of my deep knowledge of Chemistry, indeed I assure you that I have easily captured an A every term in that department. I have stood very prominently before the public this year in my capacity as Manager of the Athletic Association, where my success has been too well known to require mention. Probably you would feel favored at receiving some of my work for publication in your annual. If you have any correspondence with other schools perhaps I can help you, since I have friends in every college in the country.

　　　　　　　　　　Yours sincerely,
　　　　　　　　　　CLIFFORD BREWSTER MORRISON.

We regretfully inform our readers that, owing to the egotistic character of his bombastic productions, we were obliged to refuse Mr. Morrison's kind offer. However, we have been able to accommodate him in his search for notoriety.

Jokelets

Miss B---ks. "What is that thing that goes around on the engine, is it the captain?"
Engineer. "No, that is the governer."
Miss B---ks. "I knew it was some kind of an officer."

* * * * *

McK----t. "May I go over to the library."
Prof. T-----r. "Yes, you may go to the gymnasium."

* * * * *

Miss W----n. "What did the Romans do in England?"
Levi. "They built a road from York to Paris."

* * * * *

A. W. B. "Bill! Bill!! them boys is chewing tobacco."

* * * * *

LOST! A cap chord. Finder return to A. E. Steere.

* * * * *

Prof. T-----r. "Hoxsie, give the definition of a circle."
W. H-----e. "A straight line bounded by a hole."

* * * * *

M------n. "I have my thesis written."
Prof. "O! how nice. Hurrah for '89."

* * * * *

Cap. K--n. "Explain the position of parade rest."
Private P----ce. "Carry the right foot six inches into the rear and three feet to the right"

* * * * *

Mr. M-----e. to new Prof. "Are you going to be a prep?"

* * * * *

D------y. "May I tear the tags off my coat?"

Prof. "What are the two constituent parts of the earth's surface?"
Student. "Land and Water."
Prof. "What does land and water constitute?"
Student. "Mud."

* * * * *

Ch--e. Mr. Rodman, have you seen the assistant farmer? I can't think of his name more than 1-3 of the time and the other 1-3 I forget it.

* * * * *

Prof. (To class who have had one lesson in German) I will give you some references to read on the subject in German, I don't think that you will have any difficulty with it.

* * * * *

HURRAH FOR GENERAL SHAFTER!

* * * * *

WHAT is Jack's pet hobby?

* * * * *

A new law in Physics, as evolved in the fertile brain of one of our love lorn swains. "The angle of inclination equals the angle of affection."

* * * * *

Miss S--th. "Has anyone a watch that will tell me the time."
C. C. C. "Never mind, Miss S----, I'll watch."

* * * * *

Student. Assistant in Physics writes this sign.
"Caustic Potash
Dont *Tuch*
Poison."

* * * * *

Miss W----n. To what people do we generally ascribe hot headed qualities.
R. J. S. The Spaniards.

Grinds

Next to the originator of a good sentence is the quoter of it

"'Tis pleasure sure to see one's name in print, A book's a book, although there's nothing in't,"	The Grist
"Some are wise and some are otherwise,"	The Faculty
"E don't obey no orders unless they is his own,"	L - dd
"Much studying is a weariness to the flesh,"	A. L. R - - - - s
"'Tis time to stir him from his trance,"	A - - - - ws
"Stay, gentle creature, full of grace,"	R. E. G.
"Whose follies blazed about to all are known, And are a secret to himself alone."	L. W. K.
"Watch him with his 'air cut,"	C - - se
"Every inch that is not fool is rogue,"	H. K.
"But Shadwell never deviates into sense,"	Doc. C - - k
"Full long were his legges and ful lene, Al like a staff ther was no calf y-seene,"	M - x - n
"Give me a moustache or give me death,"	J. W - - - y
"What is it?"	P - - k - - m
"And thou art long and lank and brown As is the ribbed sea-sand,"	W - - ht - - n
"A place to be viewed from afar and not trespassed on,"	The Gym.
"All hope abandon ye who enter here,"	One of Miss W - - - - n's exams
"He had only one idea and that was wrong,"	S - - - e
"I cannot tell what the dickens his name is,"	Garabed Krekorian
"Flat burglary as ever was committed,"	Lucky Bag
"A divinity in disguise" (Pretty much so)	C. 3
"Nowher so besy a man as ther n'as And yet, he seemde besier than he was,"	Sc - - t

"The rankest compound of villainous smell that ever
offended nostril," . . . . . . Chem. Lab.
"Prithee be serious," . . . . . . G - - - b - d
"Straining harsh discords and unpleasing sharps," Cl - - - - r
"Aye, in the catalogue we pass for men," . 169 100-69
"Love is the beginning, the middle, and the
end of everything," . . . . . B - s - - - th
"Sublime tobacco, which from east to west,
Cheers the tar's labors or the Turkman's rest,
Divine in hookas, glorious in a pipe
When tipped with amber, mellow, rich and ripe ;
Like other charmers, wooing the caress
More dazzling when daring in full dress ;
Yet thy true lovers more admire by far
Thy naked beauties—give me a cigar . . . The Gooeys
"A bright little comely girl with large dark eyes,"
Miss B - - - gs
"He was one of lean body and visage," . Joe W - - - - n
"In notes by distance made more sweet,"
The singing in Chapel
"Yet I love glory, glory's a great thing," . . A. E. M.
"I do know him by his gait," . . . D - n - - ls
"This is the short and long of it," G - - d - n - r and W - - ht - - n
"A college joke to cure the dumps," . . Chase's hair cut
"Oh wad some power the giftie gie us,
To see ourselves as ithers see us," . . Preps
"There was a laughing devil in his sneer," . O - - n
"And also could you look a little modest,
'twould be convenient," . . . . M - - r - - n
"Swans sing before they die, 'twere no bad thing
Should certain persons die before they sing." Glee Club

Fearful to Contemplate

The degeneracy of H. Knowles.
The number of times Steere has said "Oh, fierce."
The lunatic career of that malicious organ, the Providence News.
The diminutive size of the average Prep.
The sporty tendencies of A. L. Reynolds.
The college church attendance on Sunday.
The career of the Bluffer.
The foxiness of a certain reverend Senior.
The shrinkage of the class of '01.
The remoteness of the time when we shall have a tennis court.
The evolution of gas by Maxson.
The internal dissensions of The Grist Editorial Board.
The enormous size that your laundry bill will attain after neglecting to pay it for a few weeks.
The senseless opposition of certain individuals toward the institution.
The airs assumed by certain martial spirits decked in a little brief authority.
The regulations in Lippitt Hall.
The proficiency of certain of our analytical chemists in guessing the contents of known solutions.
The way in which personal prejudices are sometimes vented by the improper use of public authority.
The extreme antiquity of the average College catalogue cut.

Au Revoir

And now this book is finished
 A word we have to say,
To the kind forbearing reader
 Ere our pens are laid away.

Our toil it has been heavy,
 Our troubles not a few;
But all is given freely
 If it only pleases you.

But if within these covers
 Some joke you ere should find,
Pray do not feel insulted
 By a harmless little grind.

So now to your attention
 This Grist we do present;
And give our thanks to those
 Who kindly help have lent.

We will say to the critics,
 Whose mercy we implore,
Since we perhaps may meet again,
 Not good-by, but au revoir.

Advertisements

List of Advertisers

Adams, G. A., Wakefield	21
American Type Founders Co., Boston, Mass	14
Anchor Electric Co., Boston, Mass	14
Arnold & Maine, Providence	18
B. & H. Electric Co., Providence	20
Babcock, A. T., Wakefield	24
Babcock, E. M., Wakefield	16
Babcock, G. H., Westerly	19
Barbour & Steadman, Wakefield	12
Blanding & Blanding, Providence	7
Bradley, Annie C. Wakefield	19
Bliss, L. C. & Co., Boston	16
Bates, W. L., Wakefield	22
Browne, C. L., Wakefield	22
Bureau of Civil Service, Washington, D. C	22
Covell, H. J., Wakefield	4
Clark. C. A., Wakefield	21
Clemens, Philip, Peacedale	24
Crandall, J. B. & Co., Westerly	13
Crescent Cycle Co., Wakefield, R. B	4
Dixson, L. & Co., Peace Dale	23
Easterbrooks, F. R., Peace Dale	5
Eldred Bros., Wakefield	19
Fiske, Everett O., Boston	18
Flanigan, C. A., Wakefield	21
Franklin Press, Providence	1
Gardener, Henry R., Wakefield	14
Gelb, Victor, Providence	14
Gillis' Son's, D., Wakefield	9
Greenman, A. A., Kingston	16
Grffin, D. B., Wakefield	19
Gould, W. G., Peace Dale	10
Heald & Erickson, Providence	2
Helme, B. E., Kingston	11

Hodge, E. L., Peace Dale	8
Holt, S. N., Wakefield	24
Hunt, J. J., Peacedale	6
Irons & Russell, Providence	5
Kendall Manufacturing Co., Providence	12
Kent, G. L., Wakefield	22
Kenoon, O. D., Wakefield	21
Knott, L. E. & Co., Boston, Mass	7
Lapphin, Jack & Co., Wakefield	19
Libby, A., Peace Dale	5
Leslie, Mary, Wakefield	13
Mumford, J. A., Wakefield	16
Murney, Miss L., Wakefield	9
New York Calcium Light Co., New York	20
Palmer, B. W., Wakefield	15
Peckham, Fred, Wickford	20
Pitkin, A. B. & Co., Providence	18
Pollock, W. A., Peace Dale	9
R. I. College, Kingston	3
R. I. News Co., Providence	12
R. I. Photo Engraving Co., Providence	2
Reed's Sons, Jacob, Philadelphia, Pa	7
Rider, Burnett, Providence	10
Rider, Sidney, Providence	10
Robinson, B. F., Wakefield	4
Sherman, D. W., Wakefield	16
Sheldon, G, H., Wakefield	16
Sheldon, John L., Wakefield	15
Sherman, G. C., Wakefield	9
Stillman, O., Westerly	9
Strobridge, Frank, Wickford	20
Styles, F. W., Westerly	22
Teft, James A., Wakefield	24
The Hudson Valley Creamery Butter	15
Union Teachers' Agency, Washington, D. C	8
White, Charles A., Wakefield	13
Wickford House, Wickford	4
Wilcox, B. C., Wakefield	15
Woods, Paull, Wakefield	23
Wright, S. G., Wakefield	11

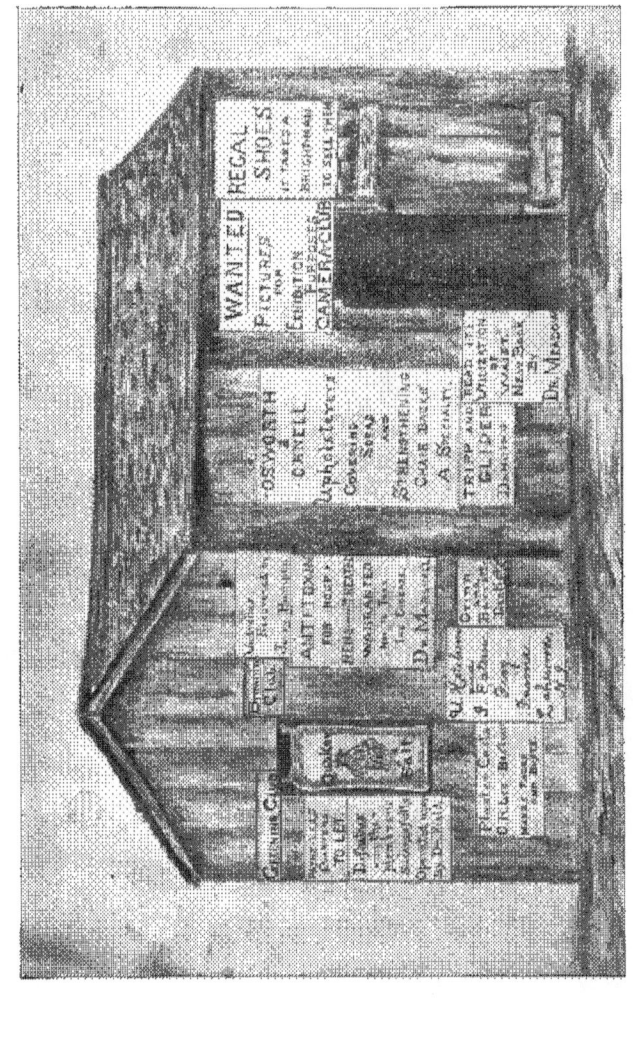

E. N. CASEY,
Treas. & Gen. Mgr.

A. C. WYER,
Secretary.

The Franklin Press Co.,

Printers and Lithographers

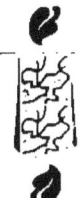

Letter Press and Process Printing of every description. Half-Tones, Wood Cuts, and Electrotypes. We have exceptional facilities for the correct execution of technical work, requiring a knowledge of School, College and University Methods.

PRINTERS OF THE '00 GRIST.

TEL. 1121

63 Washington Street   **Top Floor**

Providence, R. I.

HEALD & BRADY,
STUDIO of PHOTOGRAPHY,

—333 Westminster Street,—

PROVIDENCE, R. I.

RHODE ISLAND COLLEGE
—OF—
Agriculture and Mechanic Arts.

Technical instruction in agriculture, the mechanic arts, and the sciences. The four-year courses lead to the degree of Bachelor of Science and are six in number; the course in agriculture, in mechanics, in chemistry, in physics and mathematics, in biology, and the general course. Special courses in agriculture and mechanics. The preparatory department includes a course of one or two years according to the attainments of the students. The object of this course is to prepare students for entering the college courses.

The facilities for instruction include an excellent library, well equipped laboratories for chemistry, botany, mechanics and biology, the latter having a large collection of Rhode Island birds; and a farm embracing a large variety of soils for the departments of agriculture and horticulture.

EXPENSES.—Per year:—Room rent, $9; board, $108; fuel, $12; light, $3 to $9; books, $15 to $30; washing, $10 to $20; reading-room tax, .75; general expense, $1.50; laboratory fees, $6 to $30. Uniform, $15. Total for year,—minimum, $173; maximum, $253. Students of ability have opportunity to earn enough to pay a portion of their expenses.

EXPENSE FOR WOMEN.—Board, including room rent, $3 per week; fuel and lights supplied at cost. Rooms furnished. Other expenses as above.

Requirements for Admission to Preparatory Department, 1899: Arithmetic; geography; English grammar; United States History.

Requirements for Admission to the College, 1899: Arithmetic; algebra; plane geometry; English grammar; advanced English; United States history; geography, physical and political; one year of French, German or Latin.

Further details concerning entrance requirements, with other information, will be found in the college catalogue which may be obtained upon application to the President,

JOHN H. WASHBURN, PH. D.,
Kingston, R. I.

H. J. Covelle,

Jeweler and Optician,

MAKES A SPECIALTY OF

Fitting Glasses ♦ ♥ ♦ ♥

and

Oculists' Prescription Work.

Repairing of All Kinds.

WAKEFIELD, R. I.

ROBINSON'S

Established 1821.

WAKEFIELD, R. I.

G ROCERS ....

Imported and Domestic Fancy Groceries, Table Delicacies.

OUR SPECIALTY.

Tea, Coffee, Fancy Crackers, Cigars and Tobacco. Pillsbury's Flour, Ferris Hams and Bacon.

WICKFORD HOUSE.

Comfortable Rooms.

GOOD SHORE DINNERS OUR SPECIALTY.

----- Low Prices. -----

Mrs. Ellen D. Prentice,

WICKFORD, R. I.,

Proprietor.

We are the Oldest and Most Reliable Dealers in South Kingstown of

Bicycles and Supplies.
Cameras and Supplies.

Large and Complete Stock Constantly on Hand.

SOLE AGENTS FOR

CRESCENT and TRIBUNE Bicycles.

AUTHORIZED AGENTS FOR

Eastman Kodaks and Supplies.

RENTING.   REPAIRING.

Crescent Cycle Co.,

Opposite Depot.

WAKEFIELD, R. I.

FREDERICK R. EASTERBROOKS,

Hair Dressing and Shaving Parlor.

Dealer in Cigars, Tobacco and Cheroots.

POOL ROOM IN THE REAR.

Located in Peace Dale, R. I.

Two minutes walk from the depot

Chas. F. Irons,   Charles A. Russell

Irons & Russell,

MANUFACTURERS OF

Emblems and

College Pins,

102 FRIENDSHIP STREET,
PROVIDENCE, R. I.

..A. LIBBY...

Horse Shoeing

and

General Jobbing,

High Street,   Peace Dale, R. I.

FURNITURE!

A FULL LINE OF

Chamber Sets, Brass Trimmed Enameled Beds, with Woven Wire Springs.
Dining Tables, Chairs, Rockers, Chiffonieres, Couches, Lounges.
Carpets, Japanese and China Mattings.

WALL PAPERS WITH BORDERS TO MATCH.
Special Attention Given to Window Shade Work.

J. J. Hunt,   Peace Dale, R. I.

Blanding & Blanding,

Wholesale AND Retail Druggists,

PHYSICIANS' PRESCRIPTIONS A SPECIALTY.

54 and 58 Weybosset Street,

Providence, R. I.

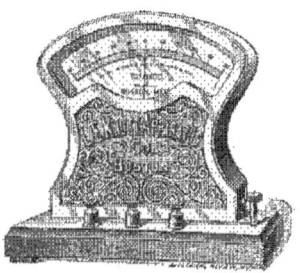

Our new $5 combined Voltameter and Ammeter shown in the above cut is giving the utmost satisfaction in storage battery and private experimental work.

MICROSCOPIC, CHEMICAL AND PHYSICAL APPARATUS.
PHOTOMETERS AND CHEMICALS.
SPECIALTY:
THE NATIONAL PHYSICS APPARATUS.

L. E. KNOTT APPARATUS CO.,
16 Ashburton Place, Boston, Mass.

JACOB REED'S SONS,
1412-1414 Chestnut St., Philadelphia.

Correct Outfittings for Young Men.

The Newest, Brightest and Best Things in

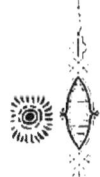

Clothing,

Furnishings,

Hats, Shoes,

Athletic Wear,

Uniforms, Etc., Etc.

TEACHERS WANTED!

Union Teachers' Agencies of America.

Rev. L. D. BASS, D. D., Manager.

 Pittsburg, Pa., Toronto, Can., New Orleans, La., New York, N. Y., Washington, D. C., San Francisco, Cal., Chicago, Ill., St. Louis, Mo., and Denver, Colorado. ♥ ♥ ♥ ♥ ♥ ♥ ♥ ♥ There are thousands of positions to be filled. We had over 8,000 vacancies the past season.

Unqualified Facilities for Placing Teachers in Every Part of the U. S. and Canada.

Address all Applications to Washington, D. C.

E. S. HODGE,
PEACE DALE, R. I.

Plumbing, Steam and Gas Fitting,

SPECIAL ATTENTION GIVEN TO

STEAM, HOT WATER AND HOT AIR

HEATING.

AGENT FOR THE FAMOUS GLENWOOD RANGES.

O. STILLMAN,

The Bookseller and Stationer,

Opp. P. O. Westerly, R. I.

Agent for Crescent, Cleveland, Keating, Featherstone, Remington, Victor, and other first-class Bicycles, and Bicycle Sundries. Eastman's Kodaks, and other makes of Cameras, with a good variety of Photographic Supplies. Golf goods of all kinds. A large stock of well seasoned Golf Balls.

The Yankee Watch, fully guaranteed, and costing only $1.00.

The Printing we do
✦✦✦✦✦

Is....

Well Done,

Promptly Done

AND

Reasonably Done.

D. Gillies' Sons,
TIMES PRINTING OFFICE,
Wakefield, R. I.

At MRS. L. MURNEY'S
A FINE ASSORTMENT OF
...Millinery...
ALWAYS ON HAND

All orders promptly attended to.
Made up Mourning Bonnets and Hats Always Ready.

Columbia Street.

Sherman's Fancy.

Best Flour On Earth.

Geo. C. Sherman,

42 and 44 High Street,

Wakefield, R. I.

W. A. POLLOCK,

Meats and Provisions.

MARKET GARDENER.

Breeder of A. J. C. C. Jerseys.

PEACE DALE, R. I.

Farm Tower Hill.

THE PEACE DALE STORE.

The Place that is Always Well Stocked with a Full Line of

DRY GOODS,   BOOTS, SHOES,   GROCERIES,
PATENT MEDICINES,   AND   CONFECTIONERY,
FRUITS,   RUBBERS.   NUTS.

(A GENERAL STORE.)

Also a Splendid Stock of Woollen Goods made by the Peace Dale Mfg. Co., consisting of Serges, Worsteds, Cassimeres, Golf and Bicycle Cloths in great variety. Send for Sample.

TELEPHONE 107-4   **W. G. GOULD, Prop.**

OLD AND RARE BOOKS,

FOR SALE BY

SIDNEY S. RIDER,

Editor and Publisher of ————

BOOK NOTES,

A Fortnightly Journal, Historical, Literary and Critical.

Second Hand Books.   **Rhode Island Genealogies.**

52 SNOW STREET, PROVIDENCE.

———ALSO———

POSTAGE STAMPS.

RARE AND VALUABLE FOREIGN AND U. S. STAMPS.

CORRESPONDENCE SOLICITED.

Burnett Rider, 52 Snow St., Providence.

IF YOU WANT TO BUY YOUR
DRUGS AND MEDICINES
At City Prices, You will call on

S. G. WRIGHT,   **WAKEFIELD, R. I,**

"It's a mighty hard position to be in."

B. E. HELME.
Kingston, R. I.
DRY • GOODS • AND • GROCERIES.

FINE CONFECTIONERY.   LOWNEY'S CHOCOLATES.

The Rhode Island News Company.

139 & 141 Westminster Street, • *Providence, R. I.*

Books : { Agricultural, Miscellaneous, Educational, Juvenile. }

Stationery : { Everything Needed For School and Office. }

Sporting Goods ; { Bicycles and Bicycle Sundries, Base Ball Goods, Tennis Goods, Fishing Tackle. }

Periodicals; { By Single Number. Subscriptions at Lowest Rates. }

LARGEST STOCK.   LOWEST PRICES.

THE RHODE ISLAND NEWS COMPANY,
139 & 141 Westminster Street, Providence, R. I.

(12)

INDUCEMENTS TO SOUTH COUNTY
BUYERS OF CLOTHING

UP TO DATE CLOTHING
♣ ♣ AND ♣ ♣
FURNISHINGS,

At 10 to 20 per cent. less than city prices. Small Expenses Enable us to do this, and with the Large Stock We Carry, you are Sure to Find what will Fit and Please.

T. B. Crandall, 10 High St., Westerly, R. I.

Henry K. Gardiner, M. D.
PHYSICIAN and SURGEON.
WAKEFIELD.
TELEPHONE 112-5.

C. A. White,
DENTIST.
MAIN STREET.
WAKEFIELD R. I

Miss Leslie,
Fashionable
DRESS MAKING.

Prices Reasonable.

Bank Building, Wakefield, R, I.

VICTOR GELB,
Caterer

CAFE ST. GEORGE　　　　**WESTMINSTER ST**

Ladies' and Gentlemen's Oyster House
121 to 125 WEYBOSSET ST.

American Type Founders Co.

easily leads the world in the production of original and useful type faces and carries in stock every requisite for the complete equipment of a printing office. An outfit can be purchased to better advantage here than at any other place simply because of the above facts and that you buy everything at once

No. 270 Congress Street
Boston, Mass., U. S. A.

PROMINENT FEATURES in Anchor Switches are:

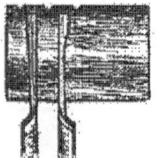

KNIFE CONTACTS
and mechanism of nickel steel

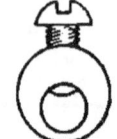

Eccentric Binding Posts
Special Springs that do not break.

Lined Covers
with voltage and capacity stamped on the front.
Insist on the genuine with an Anchor on handle and in the porcelain.

Anchor Electric Company,
Boston, Mass.
Monadnock Block, Chicago.

BUTTER.

THE HUDSON VALLEY CREAMERY BUTTER is claimed by experts to excel in quality and flavor. Same is shipped in pound prints and tubs. For sale by all first class grocers.

J. L. SHELDON,

Complete House Furnishings.

WAKEFIELD, R. I.

B. W. PALMER,

DEALER IN

Men's, Boys' and Children's

CLOTHING,

Hats, Caps, Gents' Furnishings, Bicycle Clothing.

Mens and Boys Boots and Shoes.

MAIN ST.   **WAKEFIELD, R. I.**

BICYCLE REPAIRING.

Does your bicycle need repairing. I am prepaired to guarantee first class workmanship and quote lowest possible price on all kinds of bicycle repairing.

Cone and Axle Work a specialty. Agent for the Eagle, Union, Springfield, and Club Special bicycles.

Bicycles for rent by hour, day, week and month. Full line of sundries.

B. C. WILCOX.

Columbia Corner.

WAKEFIELD R. I.

IT HAS BEEN PROVEN A FACT THAT THE

"REGAL" SHOE

Will wear as well and look better than any $5.00 or $6.00 pair of Shoes made. WHY? Oh, just read in the catalogue about the way they are Manufactured. You can procure one by sending your name to 109 Summer Street, Boston, Mass.

But I Sell the Shoe for $3.75 per pair, prepaid, "Regal" Polish 15c., Shoe Polisher, 35c. and a first-class custom-made Boot Tree for 95c.

HENRY M. BRIGHTMAN,

42 DAVIS HALL,   Special Agent College

J. A. MUMFORD,

34, 36 & 38 Main Street,
WAKEFIELD, R. I.

HACK.
BOARDING.
SALE AND
LIVERY

STABLE

The Largest Stable in Wakefield, where can be found a Large Line of Single and Double Teams, Hacks, Wagonettes, Surreys, Single and Double Carriages, Party Wagons, Etc.
Funerals, Weddings, Picnic Parties accommodated at Short Notice. Open Day and Night. Call for a "Bus" time table

TELEPHONE CONNECTION.

D. W. Shannon,

Fine

Footwear,

WAKEFIELD, R. I.

Babcock Bazaar.

DRY GOODS,
Fancy Crockery and Tinware.

E. M. BABCOCK,
WAKEFIELD R.I.

GENERAL VIEW OF R. I. C.

The Fisk Teachers' Agencies.

EVERETT O. FISK & CO., Proprietors.

4 Ashburton Place, Boston, Mass.   156 Fifth Ave., New York, N. Y.   1041 32nd St., Washington, D. C.   378 Wabash Ave., Chicago, Ill.   25 King St., West Toronto, Can.   414 Century Building, Minneapolis, Minn.   730 Cooper Building, Denver, Colo.   525 Stimson Block, Los Angeles, Calif.   420 Parrott Building, San Francisco, Calif.

Send to any of the above agencies for Agency Manual. Correspondence with employers is invited. Registration forms sent to teachers on application.

THE MAMMOTH
New . England . Grocery . and . Tea . House

93 TO 101 WEYBOSSET STREET, PROVIDENCE, R. I.

Branches at Pawtucket and Worcester

PRICE LISTS, COMPLETE TO DATE, MAILED FREE TO ANY ADDRESS.

B. F. ARNOLD   H. F. MAINE.

MACHINERY

.... AND ALL

APPURTENANCES

A. B. Pitkin Machinery Company,

39 Exchange Place, Providence, R. I.

(18)

LAPPIN'S
Ladies', Men's and Children's
..Outfitters..

Ladies' Suits, Skirts, Silk Waists, Underwear, Corsets, Hosiery, etc., The lowest price store in County.

Wakefield, R. I.   Newport, R. I.
Narragansett Pier, R. I.

SATISFACTION

It is a great satisfaction to see you wearing OUR clothing, and glad to know that you are satisfied with your purchase. It is fan to do business, but it's happiness to do business square, and the results never fail to satisfy.

A well pleased man, recommends another, and he in turn, recommends another and so on, until you find that business is coming your way.

Such is our store history. We try to do business right. Our policy is broad and liberal. No new commercial principle, having the elements of better and newer ideas, is allowed to pass. This helps us to be leaders and gives our customers better and cheaper clothing, which means, better satisfaction.

As often as possible the people shall buy here for less than anywhere else.

The Brick Mill is opposite our store.

GEO. H. BABCOCK,

16-20 Main Street,   Westerly, R. I.

Griffin's Pharmacy,
WAKEFIELD, R. I.

Pure Drugs and Medicines.

Ice Cold Soda and Mineral Waters always on draught.

FINEST CIGARS, ETC.

D. B. Griffin, - - Proprietor

ELDRED BROS.,
FIRST-CLASS

Groceries, Meats, Vegetables, Fruit, and Confectionery,

WAKEFIELD, R. I.

GEO. H. SHELDON,

Newsdealer & Stationer

Agent for Spalding Bicycles.

ALSO DEALER IN

ALL KINDS OF SPORTING GOODS.

Base Ball, Foot Ball, Golf, Tennis, and Bicycle Supplies.

188 MAIN STREET, WAKEFIELD, R. I.

MILLINERY
— AT —

Miss Annie C. Bradley's.

WESTERLY, WAKEFIELD, WICKFORD.

The Wickford
Dry Goods Store,
BRICK BLOCK, WICKFORD, R. I.

Is the place to buy Dry and Fancy Goods, Toilet Articles, Gents' Furnishings, Boots, Shoes and Rubbers, Etc.

The Best Goods at the Lowest Prices

Frank A. Peckham.

Frank O. Strobridge,

—DEALER IN—

READY MADE CLOTHING,

Hats, Caps, and Gents' Furnishings; Boots, Shoes and Rubbers.

—GREGORY BUILDING,—
WICKFORD, R. I.

B. & H.
Electric Construction
AND SUPPLY CO.,

Electric light plants installed. Motors set up and connected. Wiring of buildings and stores. Special attention given to wiring old houses.

Battery work of all kinds. Combination and electric fixtures. Electric supplies furnished on short notice.

Prompt attention and best of work.

—ESTIMATES GIVEN FREE.

Hodge Bldg., 174 Weybosset Street,

PROVIDENCE, R. I.

A. B. BROWNELL, Manager.

Take Elevator.

T. C. MURRAY. Telephone Call 211 Spring

New York Calcium Light Co.,

MANUFACTURERS OF

Pure Oxygen, Oxygen and Hydrogen Gas,

AIR COMPRESSED IN CYLINDERS.

102 Utica Street, Boston.   *309 So. 5th St., Phila.*

410 and 412 Bleecker Street, N. Y.

J. C. Barbour.   O. F. Stedman.

Dentistry

Robinson Street, Wakefield.

KENYON'S,

At Wakefield,

Is the place to buy your

DRY GOODS.

Charles A. Clarke,

DEALER IN

BOOTS, SHOES
AND
RUBBERS, HATS,
AND
CAPS AND GENTS'
FURNISHINGS.

Main St., Wakefield, R. I.

Flanagan's
Fruit Store,

Main St.,   Wakefield, R. I.

Full line of Fruits, Confectionery, Cigars and Tobacco, etc.

Drink Wakefield Mineral Water Co's. soda. Manufactured from pure spring water, Chaquot Club extracts, pure granulated sugar. No artificial sweetening; put up in thoroughly clean bottles.

C. A. FLANAGAN, Manager.

GEORGE A. ADAMS,

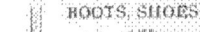

Quick Lunch
and Restaurant.
also Confectionery,
Cigars, Tobacco,
and Small Drinks.

Main Street, Wakefield, R. I.
Near Columbia Corner.

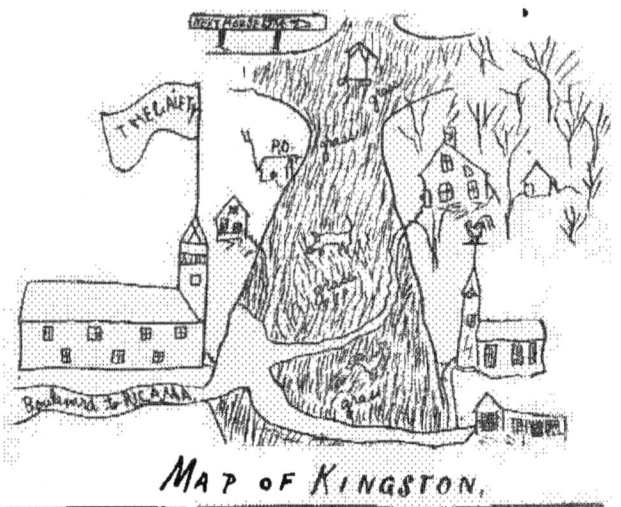

MAP OF KINGSTON.

Stiles PORTRAITS
BROWN BUILDING, WESTERLY, R. I.

THE
Narragansett Specialty Co's
BLACKING AND DRESSING
are the best for Ladies' and Gents'
black and russet shoes.
Try it and you will be convinced

W. Luther Bates, Manager.
Columbia Corner,   Wakefield, R. I.

THOROUGHBRED POULTRY
Buff Cochins

AS FINE As There Is In AMERICA.
Also LIGHT BRAHMA And PARTRIDGE
CO HINS. Exhibition Birds and Breeders
always for sale.

G. C. Kent. Wakefield, R. I.

WANT GOOD WORK?

Then work for the U. S. Gov't. Over 85,000 Positions filled through Civil Service Examinations. We teach and aid you to secure employment. Write inclosing stamp for information to

BUREAU OF CIVIL SERVICE INSTRUCTION,

STA. B, WASHINGTON, D. C.

This year there will be a slight change in the style of hair cuts. They will be as follows:

Merchant, Student, Professor, Wales, American, West Point, Pompadour, Also the English A la mode.

C. L. BROWN,

※ College Barber ※

WAKEFIELD, - - R. I.

PAUL WOODS

..Builder..

AND DEALER IN

Fine Carriages.

REPAIRING OF ALL KINDS A SPECIALTY. **Wakefield, R I.**

A. T. BABCOCK,

WAKEFIELD, R. I.

Dealer in

Ice Cream, Wholesale and Retail.

—BAKERY, CATERER.—

WRITE FOR PRICES.

PHILIP CLEMENS,

Dealer in

Glass, Tin, Iron and Wooden Ware.

Also a Nice Line of Fancy Goods

Store Opp. Congregational Church.

PEACEDALE, R. I.

JAMES A. TEFFT,

Florist and Market Gardener,

PEACE DALE, R. I.

Funeral Work of All Kinds at SHORT NOTICE.

Carnations and Violets in their season.

Decorating Plants for Rental and Sale.

House Closed on Saturday.

Miss L. Dixson & Co.,

...Millinery...

Peace Dale, R. I.

S. N. HOLT,

Keep your eye on the Crimson Rims. We are headquarters for the famous

Syracuse Bicycles.

Other grades at Low Prices. First Class Repairing.

COLUMBIA CORNER.

A. A. Greenman,

DEALER IN

Groceries, Dry Goods,

* * * *

ETC., ETC.

Kingston, R. I.